DEADLY
Roses

The 20 Year Curse

Marvin Marable

My true story about the murder of Lita McClinton Sullivan and
the investigation, arrest, trial and conviction of James Vincent Sullivan.

A GCCI PUBLICATION
GCCI, LLC 2010

Available at:
www.createspace.com/900002733
and retail stores

ISBN: 1439257477
ISBN-13: 9781439257470

To Christina Bradshaw
I hope that you enjoy
The book!

THIS BOOK IS DEDICATED TO MY FAMILY AND FRIENDS

∞

CONTENTS

∞
PHOTOGRAPHS

Pages 96 to 105

∞

FOREWORD

This book is about a former New York state trooper named Marvin D. Marable who moved to Atlanta and married Poppy Finley. Ms. Finley's best friend from Spelman College, Lita McClinton Sullivan, was married to James Vincent Sullivan. All are African-American, except Sullivan who is white.

Everything seemed to be going right for the two couples. Marvin and Poppy were both successful in their businesses, and they had recently purchased a luxury home in a million-dollar Sandy Springs neighborhood in metropolitan Atlanta. Jim and Lita had recently purchased an oceanfront mansion in Palm Beach and a luxury townhouse in the Buckhead section of Atlanta.

Jim Sullivan had moved to Macon, Georgia, from Boston in 1973 to assist his uncle Frank Bienert manage his liquor distributorship, Crown Beverages. Jim grew up on the south side of Boston and graduated from College of the Holy Cross. He met Lita during the time of his divorce from his first wife, who eventually returned to the Boston area with the couple's four children. Jim developed a strong attraction to Lita. He showered her with gifts, and then, to the surprise of many, he married her. It has been said that Lita's parents (especially her father) were not totally comfortable with Lita marrying Jim. When Jim's uncle died, Jim inherited the liquor distributorship.

Jim amassed a fortune through his shrewd operation of the liquor business and eventually became a millionaire. He purchased an ocean-front mansion in Palm Beach and he owned a Rolls Royce Corniche and other luxury automobiles. Lita was a socialite in Atlanta and Macon, but Palm Beach was a different story. Lita did not feel that she was accepted in Palm Beach because she was African-American.

As predicted by some, the marriage eventually began to fail. Charging infidelity and cruel treatment, Lita hitched a U-Haul to the back of her Mercedes SL and drove to Atlanta from Palm Beach. The next day she filed for a divorce against Jim.

Poppy and Lita began spending a great deal of time with each other after Lita moved back to Atlanta. Marvin and Poppy's marriage was also beginning to fail, and Marvin told his wife that she would also end up getting a divorce if she continued to spend so much time with Lita.

Marvin became suspicious of Poppy when he found a copy of a letter she had written to her attorney outlining what she wanted in a prospective divorce settlement against Marvin. To obtain additional information, Marvin placed a wiretap on his home telephone. He intercepted telephone calls from his wife Poppy as well as from Lita because she often used the telephone when she was at their house. Marvin contacted one of Jim's attorneys, John Taylor, for possible representation in his impending divorce, and told him about the wiretap recording. Taylor told him that Jim would be interested in hearing the tapes.

Marvin was ready to remove the recording device from his telephone, but Jim begged him to leave it in place, saying he would make it worth his while to do so. Jim was indeed very interested in the recordings and agreed to pay Marvin $30,000 if he did not have to pay any more than the $250,000 agreed to in Lita's postnuptial agreement. Against his better judgment, Marvin left the device on his telephone.

As luck would have it, Poppy and Lita found the wiretap device and turned it over to the Fulton County District Attorney's Office. Poppy then filed for a divorce against Marvin.

Even with the $250,000 postnuptial agreement, Lita was asking for a great deal more. The divorce proceedings had dragged on for over a year, and the legal fees had exceeded $100,000 with no settlement in sight.

Marvin shipped the forty wiretap tapes to Jim by courier and Jim promised not to copy the tapes, but to take notes only. Later, Marvin flew to the Palm Beach mansion to meet with Jim to discuss their divorces.

When the tapes were returned to Marvin via Jim's attorney's office, some of the tapes were missing. Marvin confronted Jim and his attorney Jeffrey Bogart, but they claimed no knowledge of the missing tapes. Marvin later heard that Jim's attorney was planning to use the missing tapes in the Sullivan divorce case. This infuriated Marvin, and he broke off all communications with Jim Sullivan.

Then one morning, just before a property settlement hearing, Lita Sullivan was brutally murdered by a gunman posing as a florist deliveryman. Pink roses littered the foyer of the elaborate townhouse in Atlanta's fashionable Buckhead community, and Lita lay mortally wounded on the floor beside them. She died enroute to the hospital or shortly afterward.

Three days before Lita's murder—and more than eight months after any contact,—Jim had made an early morning telephone call to Marvin, asking questions about Lita.

The case received immediate widespread media coverage. After the murder, there was extensive television, newspaper, magazine, and radio coverage. There was much speculation as to who committed the murder, why the murder was committed, and how it was carried out. James Sullivan and Marvin Marable were both considered prime suspects in Lita's murder.

∞

PREFACE

Writing any book is a major undertaking. Writing a book about true life events which involve the writer is an even greater undertaking. When the story involves murder and conspiracy, and the writer is a prime suspect, it opens up a whole new arena.

I knew that writing this book would be both therapeutic and emotional. But I was not ready for the need to re-live the events as they actually occurred in real life. While working on the book, I was happy and I was sad. I laughed and I cried. At some points, I was tempted to write about my life and events differently than they had actually happened, somehow thinking I could get a "do over." But unfortunately, life does not work that way; what is said is said; what is done is done; and life events cannot be changed.

As everyone does in life, I made mistakes. Decisions affect outcomes. We know the difference between right and wrong, but we do not always make the right choices. Could I have made different decisions and choices, which would have brought about different outcomes in real life? Maybe yes; maybe no.

One day, I was having lunch with my daughter Ingrid (who is now an adult; she was a child at the time of Lita Sullivan's murder). The state murder trial was about to begin, and I wanted to make her aware of some details that would come out in the trial. I told her that Jim Sullivan and I had been sharing information during our divorce proceedings. Poppy and Lita had been using the same attorney, and I had considered using Jim's attorney but decided against it. My daughter asked me, "Why would you even have anything to do with Jim?" I responded by saying, "That would be a good question if I could have predicted the future." I continued, "Obviously, I would not have had any dealings with Jim if I had known he was going to have Lita killed." I told my daughter that Jim and I had stopped communicating at least eight months before Lita was murdered. There was one exception: the call that Jim made to me just three days before Lita was murdered.

The title of the book, *Deadly Roses: The Twenty-Year Curse*, is very appropriate. For nearly twenty years, I was considered a prime suspect in Lita Sullivan's murder. I felt as if I had been cursed by society. I felt as if I had been condemned for nearly twenty years. The authorities made numerous mistakes, even associating me with career criminals. They outlined a conspiracy, showing how Jim and I supposedly arranged Lita's death. They contacted my friends and associates and my business associates regarding Lita's murder. They provided the media with false information. Some of this false and misleading information was printed in newspapers and magazines and some appeared on network television worldwide. And, much of this information remains posted on the internet.

Not one person responsible for disseminating this false and defamatory information retracted statements or apologized after they learned the truth. Not the FBI, the GBI, or the Atlanta Police Department. The only law enforcement official that apologized was not even responsible for disseminating any false information. One day, just before Jim Sullivan's trial began, I was talking on the telephone with Fulton County Assistant District Attorney Sheila Ross. I asked Ms. Ross if I were still considered a suspect in Lita's murder. Ms. Ross responded, "Mr. Marable, we [the current District Attorney administration] never considered you a suspect during our investigation." Ms. Ross then apologized for the fact that the authorities had considered me a suspect in the past. I told her that I really appreciated what she had said, but I told her that she should not be the one apologizing. Later, I received a letter from the DA's office stating that I *was not* considered a suspect in Lita's murder. I would read the letter over and over again. The letter from ADA Ross was the beginning of the end of the twenty-year curse.

I forgive everyone who suspected that I was somehow involved with the murder of Lita McClinton Sullivan. If I had had the slightest suspicion of Jim's intentions, I would have reported him to the authorities.

I truly hope that you enjoy reading this book, and as you read, I would like for you to try and put yourself in my place. I would like for you to experience what I endured for nearly twenty years.

Sincerely,

Marvin D. Marable

∞

ACKNOWLEDGEMENTS

There are many people who helped me get through the twenty-year curse. True friends and family members already knew my character; therefore, they sought no information regarding my guilt or my innocence. They were concerned about my well-being. They would lend an ear to listen or offer an arm to lean on; they were there for me. I cannot list all of the people that supported me during my time of need, but I give special thanks to the following:

My mother, Maude S. Glaze; my wife Heather Jones-Marable; my stepfather, Henry L. Glaze (deceased); my father, Earl C. Marable (deceased) and his wife, Grace Marable; my brothers, Lawrence B. Marable, Larry C. Marable and James B. Harris; My aunt, Priscilla (Sis) Edmunds; My aunt, Erie Davis (deceased); My nephew, Gregory D. Marable; My mother's closest friend, Dora Mitchell and the rest of my family.

I would also like to thank: Renee Guy, George and Maureen Kruythoff, Stephany Davis, Yvonne LeClair, Shirley Simmons, and Clarence Williamson.

A special thanks goes to my attorney Michael Mears.

A special thanks to Pastor Melvin Fuller of the White Oak Grove Baptist Church in Sutherlin, Virginia. On many occasions I visited the church where I first attended in the small community of White Oak. To my knowledge Pastor Fuller was unaware of the details regarding the death of Lita Sullivan. However, every time I attended church in White Oak, it seemed as if Pastor Fuller's inspirational sermons were specifically tailored for me and my situation, and they were comforting. I would also like to thank the White Oak Grove Baptist Church community for their unknowing support and comfort.

And a very, very special thanks goes to my wonderful daughter, Ingrid Alexandria Marable, aka Plum Pie. Although Ingrid was too young at that time to know what was going on, she gave me a great deal of support by giving me a hug and saying, "I love you, Daddy."

∞

CHAPTER 1: THE BEGINNING

On February 5, 1987 at 2:00 p.m., I walked into the office of the Atlanta Police Department's Homicide Division on Ponce de Leon Avenue, accompanied by my attorney Mike Mears. We were greeted by homicide Detective Welcome Harris and Lieutenant Horace Walker, who ushered us into a meeting room which had a long rectangular table covered with files and other paperwork arranged in stacks. Detective Harris introduced himself and Lt. Walker and asked us to be seated. I noticed that Detective Harris's demeanor appeared to be cold and reserved, definitely not cordial. I did not know him; therefore, this could have been his normal behavior.

Detective Harris began the meeting by saying, "Mr. Marable, we asked you to come down to our office so that we could ask you some questions regarding the murder of Lita Sullivan. But first I would like to read something to you." He handed me a piece of paper containing a signature block, then began reading from another piece of paper. "You have the right to remain silent. Anything that you say can and will be used against you in a court of law. You have the right to have an attorney present before any questioning. If you cannot afford an attorney, one will be appointed to represent you before questioning. Do you understand these rights? If so, I would like for you to sign the paper acknowledging that you have been read your rights and that you understand them."

Mike and I just looked at each other in shock, and he reached for the paper. Mike said, "I am counsel for Mr. Marable, and as his attorney, I am advising him to exercise his Fifth Amendment rights." Mike then added, "This concludes this interview." Detective Harris then began asking a series of questions as if he did not hear my attorney's statement; and each time Mike advised him that I was asserting my Fifth Amendment rights.

Detective Harris let out a disappointed sigh as he began gathering his papers. Mike and I got up and headed for the door. Detective Harris then said, "Mr. Marable, you forgot your coat." I picked up my coat and Mike and I left the building.

Mike said, "They think you did it. They think that you killed Lita Sullivan!"

"Why do they think that I had something to do with Lita's murder?" I asked.

"It probably has something to do with the telephone call that Jim Sullivan made to you on January 13th, just three days before Lita was murdered," replied Mike.

"Here I'm thinking they wanted to routinely interview me because I knew Lita, but instead, they consider me a suspect."

Mike turned to me with a serious look on his face and said, "Marvin, don't discuss the phone call or anything else pertaining to this case with anyone."

I acknowledged by nodding in affirmation. Thus began the saga of "Deadly Roses: The Twenty Year Curse."

* * *

A few weeks earlier, on January 16, 1987, An African-American socialite, Lita McClinton Sullivan, was shot to death when she opened her door to a gunman posing as a florist's deliveryman.

The gunman handed her a dozen pink roses, then fired two bullets from a 9 mm automatic handgun. One of the bullets struck Lita in the head, and she died enroute to the hospital or shortly afterward.

An important property-settlement hearing relating to the postnuptial agreement had been scheduled for later that day. Lita was in the middle of a bitter and highly contested divorce case. Lita's estranged husband, millionaire James Vincent Sullivan, became one of the prime suspects, even though he was at their 13,000-plus square foot mansion in Palm Beach, Florida, when she was murdered.

What are the circumstances that led to me being considered a prime suspect in the murder of Lita Sullivan? Where do I begin?

* * *

I was born in rural Halifax County, Virginia. My parents divorced when I was a little over a year old. My mother moved to New York, and my two brothers and I stayed with my grandmother on the farm in Halifax.

My mother later remarried and my brothers and I moved to White Plains, New York, to live with her and our stepfather. After living for several years in White Plains, we moved to Mount Vernon, New York. We lived in the middle-class neighborhood of Vernon Heights, also known as "The Heights."

After I graduated from Mount Vernon High School, I worked for a few years as a cable splicing technician with the New York Telephone Company and then served in the Army and Army National Guard. I then worked as a patrolman for the Mount Vernon Police Department for a few years before being appointed as a state trooper with the New York State Police. While with the state police, I was assigned to the Drug Enforcement Administration's (DEA) Task Force. I was injured in the line of duty and eventually retired from service.

I graduated from Iona College in New Rochelle, New York and afterwards accepted a position with J.P. Stevens & Co., Inc., a textile manufacturer. After completing the training program, I was transferred to Chicago.

One of my best friends since grade school, Allen (Al) Norman, married Lita Sullivan's first cousin Cortesia (Cort). One day, while visiting with Al and Cort, I mentioned to Al that I was thinking of moving from Chicago to Atlanta. Al told me that Cort had relatives in Atlanta, Emory and JoAnn McClinton. Emory McClinton and Valencia, Cort's mother, were brother and sister. Al also mentioned that one of the McClintons' daughters, Lita, was married to a millionaire named James Vincent Sullivan, who owned a liquor distributorship. Al and Cort gave me the McClintons' address and telephone number. They called the McClintons and told them to expect a call from me during a future trip to Atlanta.

Several weeks later, I went to Atlanta to close on the purchase of a forty-four unit apartment complex. I called the McClintons and they invited me to come by and visit with them. When I arrived, JoAnn McClinton answered the door. Emory McClinton, Sr. had just returned home after playing tennis. I introduced myself and was welcomed into their home. I found the McClintons to be very warm and cordial. Mr. McClinton was an official with the U.S. Department of Transportation and Mrs. McClinton was active in the Atlanta political arena. I visited with them for several hours and we talked about everything from living in Atlanta to real estate to politics.

I occasionally visited the McClintons during my weekend trips to Atlanta. During one weekend visit, I met their daughter Lita and her husband Jim. Lita was an intelligent, charming, attractive young lady with sophistication and charisma. She had an effervescent personality. Jim appeared to be rather stern and stiff and had a heavy Boston accent. I visited with the McClintons and the Sullivans for about an hour, and we had a very enjoyable conversation.

Several weeks later, I was visiting the McClintons again, and Lita was there. During my visit, Lita's friend Poppy Finley stopped by to see her. Lita and Poppy were best friends from Spelman College in Atlanta. Lita introduced me to Poppy, an intelligent, attractive and sophisticated African-American young lady. I will always remember that Poppy had braces on her teeth and was wearing fitted jeans. I would later refer to her as *Braces and blue jeans*! Lita mentioned that Poppy was an Allstate Insurance agent, and that she could possibly insure my apartment complex. I asked for her card and told her that I would call her with the information on the apartments. When I returned to

Chicago I gave Poppy a call for an insurance quote on the apartment complex, and eventually I insured the apartments with Allstate.

While living in Chicago, I contacted a high school friend, Derrick Warner, who had relocated to the Chicago area from Mount Vernon a year or so earlier. Derrick was a scientist who worked at Argonne National Laboratory. We occasionally attended social functions in downtown Chicago. Our favorite hangout on Friday after work was a club called Dingbats. Strange name, but it was a very nice club. I met "Mr. T" at Dingbats, where he worked as a manager and a bouncer.

A management trainee from the J.P. Steven's corporate office in New York came out to Chicago to work with me for a week in my territory. During one of my conversations with her, she mentioned that she had a college friend living and working in the Chicago area. She asked me to give her friend a call sometime, because she did not know anyone in Chicago. She gave me the number, and I said I would call her.

One day I mentioned to Derrick that I was supposed to call the young lady, whose name was Dolores Williamson. We joked about how she would look, and Derrick knew I had reservations about blind dates. I eventually called Dolores, who was originally from Noank, Connecticut, near the submarine base in Groton. I told her that I would stop by on the upcoming Saturday, if it suited her schedule. I also told her that I would probably bring a friend, Derrick. (This way if I did not like her, it would not appear to be a date.)

Saturday rolled around and Derrick and I were on our way to Dolores's apartment. We again joked about how she would look, and we each said, "You can have her!" We walked up to her apartment door and I rang the doorbell. She opened the door—and Derrick and I just stared at her, speechless! We introduced ourselves and she invited us in. Dolores was a very attractive African-American woman with beautiful green eyes. We watched television and talked for a while. When Dolores went into the kitchen (and out of our sight), Derrick and I began whispering to each other in a joking manner. I said, "She's mine. I knew her first!" Derrick replied, "No, she's mine, you were hesitant to even call her!" When Dolores returned to the living room, we abruptly stopped joking and both smiled at her.

Dolores and I talked frequently, and eventually began dating. One evening, Dolores was at my apartment in Clarendon Hills when a former girlfriend from New York called. Renee Guy and I had once been engaged, but we broke off the engagement. Renee was hopeful that we would eventually get back together, but the breakup had been traumatic for me, and I was not so optimistic. I told Renee that I could not talk at that time because I was entertaining a guest. Renee became very upset and demanded to know who I was entertaining. My answers were vague, initially, but when she continued to question me I finally admitted that I was dating someone.

I could see that Dolores was becoming uncomfortable. Renee continued to ask probing questions, and I finally told her that I would have to hang up. Renee then said, "I'm coming out there!" and hung up the phone! I sat there for a few moments just holding the telephone. Dolores looked at me and asked, "What's wrong?" I hesitated for a few moments and then said, "My former fiancée threatened to come out here from New York!" Dolores said, "I'd better go."

"You don't have to go. Besides, Renee is all the way in New York. It would take her at least five or six hours to get here. She would have to pack, book a flight, get to the airport, fly to Chicago, rent a car, and then drive to Clarendon Hills. She has my address, but she doesn't know how to get here. Besides, she was just bluffing!"

Dolores looked at me with a serious, concerned expression on her face. "What if she is already in Chicago, and she does know where you live? I'm leaving now!" I walked Dolores to her car—and I looked around the parking lot for any unfamiliar vehicles.

Dolores and I continued to date, and the relationship became serious. I told Dolores that I was thinking about moving to Atlanta and that I wanted her to move down after I got settled in. She seemed interested but did not give me a definite answer. I could understand her hesitation, because she was just beginning her career in Chicago.

During the next Thanksgiving holiday, Dolores and I decided to visit our families in New York and Connecticut. We arrived in New

York on the Wednesday before Thanksgiving. I introduced Dolores to my mother, stepfather, and other family members. We stayed at my parents' home overnight and planned to leave for Noank, Connecticut, on Thanksgiving Day.

The next morning, I was on my way downstairs when I heard the doorbell ring. Just before reaching the bottom of the stairs, I heard my mother say, "Renee, how are you!" I stopped in my tracks on the bottom landing of the stairs, out of sight from the front door. Dolores was still upstairs in the guest bedroom (hopefully still sleeping). My mother invited Renee inside the house, and as my stepfather and mother were greeting her, I began quietly backing up the stairs. My mother walked over to the stairs and was about to walk up, when she saw me backing up. She looked at me in desperation and whispered, "Renee is here!" I looked at her and said, "I know!" I turned around and continued up the stairs. I knocked on the door and advised Dolores that Renee was downstairs and that she might want to remain upstairs until Renee left. Needless to say, Dolores did not appear to be happy about the situation.

I took a deep breath and walked back downstairs and went into the living room and greeted her. "Hi, Renee!"

She looked at me with a smile and said, "Hi, *Marabell!*" (which is how she and many other New Yorkers pronounced my last name). I walked towards her, smiled, and we embraced. Renee visited with my family and me for about forty-five minutes, after which I walked her to the door and we again embraced. She looked at me and said. "It's good seeing you again, *Marabell*. Give me a call sometime."

"I will," I replied.

I went into the kitchen where my mother was preparing the Thanksgiving dinner. My mother looked at me sternly. "You almost caused me to have a heart attack!" I just shook my head, and I am sure that I had a perplexed look on my face as I dealt with my emotions pertaining to the relationship that Renee and I once had. My mother then asked me, "Do you know what you're doing?"

I looked back at her and said, "No." She just shook her head.

Dolores and I left later that day, heading to her parents' home in Connecticut. We were greeted by Dolores's family: her mother, father, three sisters, her brother, and a brother-in-law. Her mother was very warm and friendly, and her father was cordial but reserved. I had the feeling that he was trying to size me up, to see if I was good enough for his daughter.

Dinner was served and everything was delicious. Afterward, Dolores's parents, Dolores, and I were the only ones left at the table. Dolores then looked at both of her parents and said, "Mom, Dad, there's something I want to tell you." I almost choked on my beverage, not knowing what Dolores was going to say. I had an idea, but I was not sure, but I had definitely been caught off guard. Dolores then continued, "Marvin is moving to Atlanta, and I am going to move down with him." At that point, I just wanted to disappear. I glanced at both of her parents. Before either of them could respond, Dolores added, "I know this seems like a hasty decision, but I have given it a lot of thought, and that's what I want to do." I waited for a response.

"What about your job?" her father asked. "Where are you going to work?"

Dolores said that she intended to get a job in Atlanta before she moved. The discussion continued for about ten minutes, without a negative or positive indication on her parents' position regarding Dolores's move to Atlanta.

After we left the dinner table, Mr. Williamson and I ended up in the living room alone. As we were taking, I still had the feeling that he was trying to figure out what type of person his daughter was dating and if he was good enough for his daughter. Mr. Williamson shared information with me about his career in the Navy and I shared some information about myself with him. Eventually, it was time for Dolores and me to leave. Before we departed, Mr. Williamson looked at me. "Take care of my little girl!" With a stern, serious, but respectful voice, he added, "If there are any problems, give me a call."

"I'll take care of her, and I *will* call you if there are any problems," I responded. We shook hands. Then I embraced everyone before we departed.

CHAPTER 2: THE MOVE TO ATLANTA

Moving day was in the middle of winter and in the middle of a blizzard. Toward the end of the blizzard, there was a deep freeze, and the temperature ranged from forty to fifty degrees below zero, wind chill! Chi-Town was living up to its reputation. Going from an inside temperature of seventy degrees to an outside wind chill temperature of fifty below is a shock to the system. It literally takes your breath away!

I had leased an apartment in the Peachtree North Apartments, located on North Avenue near Peachtree Street and close to downtown. Maynard Jackson, the mayor of Atlanta, lived in the building with his wife, Valerie, and I would occasionally see them entering or leaving the building. The building was secure and had a doorman on duty around the clock. It was also conveniently located for me, and only two blocks from the historic Fox Theater. Initially, I spent most of my time with real estate-related business. I hired a real estate management company to manage my apartment complex, which enabled me to pursue other ventures.

Dolores and I talked regularly on the telephone, and she was anxious to move to Atlanta. Several weeks had passed since I'd moved, but Dolores was having difficulty securing employment while still living in Chicago. One evening, she called and told me that she wanted to go ahead and move to Atlanta and then find a job. I told her that I felt it would be better if she found a job before she moved to Atlanta. She said she had been talking to her friends, and they told her that if I really cared for her, I would want her to move down now. I told her that I still felt that she should wait until she got a job, but if she really wanted to move down first, it would be okay with me. Several weeks later, Dolores moved from Chicago to Atlanta and began searching for employment. Initially, she was frustrated in her job search, but she was eventually successful in securing a position with Harland, the check-printing company.

Although I was not looking for a job, the personnel agency that placed Dolores with Harland asked me if I would be interested in a position with Avon Products, Inc. My first response was, "Doing what, selling Avon?" The recruiter assured me that I would not be selling Avon, but rather working in an entry-level management position, supervising Avon employees in the company's distribution center. I was interviewed and subsequently hired to work in Avon's distribution center in Dunwoody, a nearby northern suburb of Atlanta. Although I was working full time, I still had sufficient time to pursue my real estate interests and other business endeavors.

I met many of Atlanta's elite by attending fundraising and other social functions. Atlanta's social circle was a very tight-knit community, and it took time to get into the inner circle. In addition to meeting Mayor Jackson, I met a number of federal, state, and local officials. I quickly learned that it's not necessarily what you know but a combination of what you know and who you know. Knowing the right person can cut through a lot of so-called red tape. I invested in a number of real estate projects in Atlanta and the surrounding suburbs, as well as Hilton Head Island, South Carolina.

Dolores and I attended an engagement party for the McClintons' other daughter, Valencia. She was engaged to marry Jeffrey Weiner from New York. As Dolores and I walked from the parking lot to the entrance, she noticed Poppy Finley's Mercedes SL and said, "There's your friend's car."

Based on the tone of her voice, I just responded, "Uhm." Dolores had met Poppy on at least one occasion and she knew that she was insuring my real estate holdings.

Once inside, I introduced Dolores to the McClintons, Lita and Jim Sullivan, Jeffrey Weiner and Valencia McClinton, and other guests. We were also introduced to a number of people that I hadn't met before. I spoke with Poppy Finley briefly and told her that I would give her a call soon. While socializing with Lita and Jim, I could not help but notice how Jim was staring at Dolores. It was quite obvious to me by now that Jim liked attractive African-American women, and Dolores certainly was a prime example. An avid tennis player, Dolores was also in excellent shape. One day, while Dolores was shopping at Lenox Mall, a Leggs Pantyhose representative approached her and asked her to do a Leggs commercial. Dolores accepted, and the commercial was on the air all over the country.

∞

CHAPTER 3: DATING, MARRIAGE, AND EUROPEAN HONEYMOON

Dolores was successful in her position with Harland, but our relationship had become strained, and we soon parted ways, without animosity or resentment. Dolores and I remained friends.

A friend of mine, Sylvia Dale Mason (now Cochran), had recently given me a brochure advertising an upcoming federal government trade fair—a good opportunity for me to learn about doing business with the federal government. I began researching some of the products purchased by the federal government and learned that they purchased nearly everything that I could imagine.

I would occasionally see Poppy Finley in connection with my real estate investments and sometimes at social events. Eventually, I asked her out and we began dating. One evening, Poppy and I were having dinner at an exclusive Buckhead restaurant with Lita and Jim Sullivan. During our conversation, I mentioned to Jim that I was considering starting a business. Jim said that the best type of business would be a distributorship (the middleman), as opposed to a manufacturer (or producer). We agreed to discuss my business aspirations during a future visit to the Sullivan's residence on Nottingham Drive in Macon.

After dinner, Jim lit an expensive cigar as we were enjoying an after-dinner drink. Couples at a nearby table had been staring at our table (which was situated in the middle of the dining area) all evening. Shortly after Jim lit the cigar, the maitre d' came over to our table and politely asked Jim to extinguish it, due to customer complaints. I personally felt that the issue was more racial than Jim smoking a cigar. Jim was upset, but he complied with the request and put out his cigar.

When the waiter brought our check, Jim reached for it, but I told him I'd like to pay for half of the bill. Jim insisted on paying for the entire check and reached for his wallet. I took a credit card out of my wallet as a gesture, but Jim insisted on paying for the entire bill as he pulled several $100-dollar bills from his wallet. I said, "I see that you believe in paying cash."

Jim replied in a whisper, "If you use cash, it cannot be traced."

What a peculiar comment, I thought. I asked myself why he would make such a statement.

As I said earlier, Jim was a stern, stiff individual who appeared to be in a serious frame of mind most of the time. If he laughed, you could be sure that he was laughing about something that had been said about someone else, and not him. Jim was intelligent, but he put on the facade of knowing everything about everything. Sometimes it seemed that he tried to belittle people by attempting to intimidate them with his intelligence. His attitude appeared to say, "I am an authority in the subject at hand, and there is no way that you could possibly know more than I do!"

Lita and Jim invited Poppy and me to have dinner at their home in Macon. Poppy and I arrived at the Sullivan's home on Nottingham Drive early in the afternoon. The French provincial-style home was located in one of Macon's most exclusive neighborhoods, Shirley Hills, and its acreage backed up to the Ocmulgee River. The property was generous and private and included a large pool and pool house in a garden setting. Dinner was served in the formal dining room. The chandelier was an antique gas chandelier converted to electricity. Jim had a server bring in the various dishes from the kitchen to the dining room. Whenever Jim needed anything, he would ring a bell to summon the server. The filet mignon was so rare that bright red blood ran out when it was sliced. I politely asked for my steak to be prepared medium to medium well. Jim rang the bell and the server promptly took the steak back to the kitchen.

After dinner, Jim and I went to the parlor, and Poppy and Lita went to the sewing room. Jim offered me a cigar, but I declined. Jim selected one and clipped the end before lighting it. We then discussed the type of business I was going to establish. Jim had graduated from College of the Holy Cross in Worcester, Massachusetts, with a degree in economics. With his evident business success, I felt that he would be a good person to talk with about getting my business started. Jim again emphasized the pluses of owning a distributorship verses a manufacturing or production operation. What he told me was very helpful to me later on.

I attended the federal government trade fair that Sylvia Dale Mason had told me about, meeting many contracting officers from various federal agencies, including the General Services Administration (GSA), Department of Defense (DOD), The Department of Justice (DOJ), and the Federal Bureau of Prisons (FBP), which is a part of the DOJ. I asked as many questions as I could and obtained business cards for future contact.

Shortly after the trade fair, I resigned from Avon and incorporated Bel-Mar Corporation. I leased office space on Gordon Street in southwest Atlanta and later leased a warehouse in Decatur, Georgia. My target market was going to be the food service, lodging, and health care industries. The products I would market would support those industries and would include linens, apparel, disposables, paper products, large and small appliances, and some small electronic items.

I contacted manufacturers, including my former employer J.P. Stevens, as well as General Electric, Black and Decker, White Westinghouse, and others, and established distribution agreements with them. I began banking with the Citizens and Southern (C&S) Bank. I then began researching federal government contracts for the items I selected. It took me nearly six months to obtain my first government bid contract with GSA, and it was not easy, but I learned a great deal in the process, and it was worth it. The contract was for the huck-weave hand towel (the towel used in hospital operating rooms), and it was worth over half a million dollars.

Later that year, I had a home built on Flamingo Drive in southwest Atlanta. One day I was in the office, reviewing a bid for the Federal Bureau of Prisons, when I received a telephone call from my home alarm company advising me that the alarm at my residence has been tripped. The house was set way back off the road on top of a hill, and was secluded. When I arrived at the house, an Atlanta police officer was already on the scene. A burglar had attempted to enter the residence but was scared off when the alarm tripped. The only damage was a broken window in the breakfast room. The police officer was still conducting his investigation when I remembered that the bid I'd been working on when I got the call was due at 2:00! I had lost track of time, and I had to deliver the bid to the United States Penitentiary-Atlanta before the deadline. I said to the officer, "I've got to go now. I have a bid that's due, and I've got to leave right now!"

The officer said, "I'm not finished with my investigation."

I pulled out my business card and wrote my contact phone numbers on the back of the card. "I'll call you later," I said, "or you can call me after 2:00, but it is imperative that I leave right now."

"What about the broken window?" he asked.

"I'll reset the alarm and call someone to come and replace the window."

I made a mad dash for my Mercedes and headed down Flamingo Drive at breakneck speed. Fortunately, the bid solicitation paperwork was already completed and in my car.

I arrived at the prison just five minutes before two. Within five minutes, I had to park my vehicle, walk through the parking lot to the entrance gate into the main building, call the contracting officer, E.T. Walden, on the telephone, and physically deliver the bid to him. I parked my car and began running towards the main gate—big mistake. All of a sudden, I heard a voice come over the PA system from the main gun tower. "You! Stop running. What is your business here?"

I stopped running, and said, "I have a bid to turn in before 2:00."

The voice replied, "Proceed, but do not run."

Once inside, I had to call Walden on the house phone, but that phone was being used. I had only three minutes left before the bid closed. I turned to the person talking on the house phone. "I need to use the phone right now."

The man looked at me and said, "No speak English."

I pointed to my watch and then to the phone and said, "I need to use the phone right now, this is an emergency! *Emergencia! Por favor!* I then reached towards the telephone. He said a few more words and then hung up the phone. *"Muchas gracias!"* I said. I dialed the number to the contracting office. The phone rang several times before Walden answered. "Mr. Walden, this is Marvin Marable with Bel-Mar Corporation, I have a bid to turn in today that's due at 2:00." I looked at my watch. It was about a minute and a half before 2:00.

"Marvin, that bid was due yesterday," Walden said.

I was in shock and speechless. But then he said, "I'm only kidding. I'll be right up to get the bid." I was still in shock and I simply said, "Okay."

Several weeks later, while vacationing on Hilton Head Island, I called my office to check my messages while I was waiting for my lunch to be served. My assistant advised me that Walden had called and wanted me to call him as soon as possible. I returned the call, and he asked me a few questions. Then he asked me if I had a pen and a piece of paper and proceeded to give me a series of alphanumerics, which I wrote on the back of my business card. "What are these numbers for?" I asked.

Walden said, "Congratulations, that is your contract number, when can you begin shipping?"

I was silent for a few moments and then asked, "Are you kidding?"

"No, I'm not kidding. I'll be putting the contract and some purchase orders in the mail tomorrow."

"Thank you, Mr. Walden, thank you!" I said. The contract was worth over $1 million!

I don't want anyone to get the wrong impression and think that these contracts were handed to me on a silver platter, because they were not. I worked extremely hard to develop my business. Initially, I worked seven days a week. I would even spend several hours in the office on Sundays after church. I coined a saying: "The headaches are mine, but so are the receivables!"

* * *

One Saturday afternoon, I was at home working in the backyard when my neighbor, Sheila Maddox, stopped by to see me. I took a break and Sheila and I went into the family room. I went back outside to the get something from the backyard, and while I was out there, Sheila came to the back door and yelled, "Telephone." I walked inside expecting to hear the phone ringing, but to my surprise, the telephone receiver was laying on the end table. Sheila had answered the telephone. Who could it be? As I walked over to the phone, I noticed that Sheila was smiling. I picked up the phone and said, "Hello."

It was Poppy! She asked, "Who answered your telephone?"

I hesitated for a few seconds. "Her name is Sheila." I continued talking with Poppy, asking her how she was doing, etc.

Poppy then asked, "Who is Sheila?" in a curiously inquisitive voice.

"Sheila is my neighbor, and she lives next door; she stopped by to say hello. Her father is Councilman Maddox." Poppy knew Maddox because Poppy's cousin Morris Finley was also a city councilman in Atlanta. Poppy did not seem pleased that my neighbor stopped by to say hello and had answered my telephone.

My business continued to grow. I leased a larger office space in Decatur, near my warehouse. I also acquired additional real estate holdings, including a custom-built 6,000 square foot California contemporary ranch style home on ten acres in Ellenwood, Georgia. The home had a stable with a riding trail, a lake, and a heated swimming pool. I liked the property so much that I decided to reside there. Coming home after work was like going to a retreat.

I frequently traveled throughout the United States seeking new customers and developing new distributorship agreements with manufacturers. I also became politically active, supporting political officials on the federal, state, and local government levels. Some of the officials included U.S. Senator Sam Nunn, Congressman Wyche Fowler, and Atlanta Mayor Andrew Young. I regularly attended fundraisers and other charitable events. I even volunteered for a Junior Achievement project. Establishing political affiliations made good business sense, and I sometimes entertained the thought of running for public office myself.

I would also occasionally go to some of the local clubs, such as Ciscos and Mr. V's in southwest Atlanta, Mr. V's on Peachtree, and Dailey's, a popular restaurant located in downtown Atlanta.

An attorney friend of mine, James Booker, and I purchased some real estate properties on Hilton Head Island in South Carolina, and we occasionally went down there for weekends and vacations. I had met James through my friend Derrick Warner. Derrick and James had attended the University of Georgia together. Booker, as most people called him, handled all of my legal affairs. Another friend, Dexter Todmann, who grew up in Mount Vernon, was now living in Atlanta; Dexter (or Dr. Todmann), a graduate of Johns Hopkins University Medical School, was now practicing medicine there. The three of us would occasionally hang out at one of Atlanta's after-work spots. We were the Doctor, the Lawyer, and Indian Chief. Well, not exactly a "chief," but my heritage on both my mother's and father's side traces back to the Cherokee and Black Foot Native American tribes. So I am part Indian, but not quite a chief, unless CEO counts!

All three of us were very good at our jobs. We worked extremely hard during the week and we looked forward to an occasional Friday happy hour together. We mostly relaxed, talked and enjoyed looking at some of Atlanta's beauties.

* * *

The relationship between Poppy and me had become quite serious, and we had discussed the possibility of becoming engaged. During the next Christmas holiday, Poppy and I went to visit my parents in Mount Vernon, and I went down to Manhattan before Christmas looking for an engagement ring. I went to the diamond district, which was located only a few blocks from my old employer, J.P. Stevens. Unfortunately, I could not find the ring I was looking for in time to present it to Poppy at Christmas. When Poppy and I exchanged gifts, I could tell she was disappointed. I am pretty sure she was expecting an engagement ring.

The day after Christmas, I returned to the diamond district. I spent nearly the entire day going from jewelry wholesaler to jewelry wholesaler. Finally, I found the ring I was searching for. It was a near two-carat, round, all but flawless diamond ring. The stone was set in a platinum frame, and it was rated VVSI. The ring had a large baguette on each side of the main diamond. I had the ring appraised by an independent, certified gemologist who valued the ring for nearly double the asking price of the wholesaler. I then negotiated a reasonable price and purchased the ring.

After an exhausting day, I stopped at a local pub and had a drink before I headed home. I then took the Stamford local commuter train back to Mount Vernon. I kept my hand in my pocket, holding on to the ring inside the box. I definitely did not want to lose it! I arrived back at my parents' house and went upstairs to the guest bedroom where Poppy was staying. I was holding the ring in its case behind my back. I walked over to Poppy and said, "Poppy, will you marry me?" As I said this, I opened the ring box and presented her the ring.

Poppy hesitated, and seemed overcome by emotion. Then she answered, "Yes, I will marry you!"

When we returned to Atlanta, Poppy and Lita began planning the engagement party and the wedding. I suggested getting married in August, but I was overruled, and a date was set for May the 8th 1982. Lita and Jim gave Poppy and me an engagement party at Callanwolde Fine Arts Center. Lots of family and friends attended.

A few days after the engagement party, I received a call from a female friend who gave me some information about Jim. My friend advised me that Jim had been flirting with one of my married friends and had made a pass at her. I wanted to say something to Jim about the incident, but I had to promise my friend that I would not say anything. I thought it was very disrespectful of Jim to try to pick up a married woman whom I had invited to the engagement party—not to mention the fact that he was married, and Lita was present. Although I was tempted, I kept my word and did not say anything to Jim about the incident.

I was beginning to formulate an opinion about Jim. He seemed to feel that he was superior to everyone, and that supposedly gave him the right to treat people any way he wanted. I remember one afternoon when Poppy and I were visiting Lita and Jim, he brought his Irish wolfhound outside. Shamus was a long, lean dog with huge paws. As Poppy and I were getting ready to leave, I walked over to my Mercedes. Jim was standing next to my car with Shamus, and I made it perfectly clear to Jim that I did not want the dog in my car. I opened the rear door of my car, and before I knew it, Jim motioned for Shamus to get in the back seat. Shamus hopped into the back seat, tracking dirt on the seat with his paws. Jim began laughing— he thought it was funny. I turned to Jim and said, "Get that dog out of my car, now!" The smile quickly dropped off of Jim's face. It was obvious that he was not accustomed to anyone giving him orders or instructions, and maybe especially an African-American. But Jim tried to act as if he was not bothered as he took Shamus out of the back seat.

The months seemed to hurry by and the wedding date was soon approaching. There were three possible choices for my best man. Al Norman, my longtime friend from Mount Vernon, George Kruythoff, a very good friend that I met while working at J.P. Stevens, and James Booker, my friend who worked for the prestigious law firm of Kutak, Rock and Huie. I decided to pick James Booker.

A few days before the wedding, James gave me a bachelor party, and what a bachelor party it was. The only thing I can say is that we ran out of dollar bills and had to send out for more "ones." I have no further comment!

At last, the big day had arrived. The wedding was held at Sisters Chapel on the Spelman College Campus. The chapel was named in honor of two sisters, Laura Spelman Rockefeller and her sister Lucy Spelman, who were the mother and aunt of John D. Rockefeller, Jr. Many family members and friends from both sides of our families were in attendance, from all over the United States. I arrived at the chapel early; after all, I did not want to be late for my own wedding.

The first thing I noticed about Sisters Chapel is that it was not air conditioned. Although May is not nearly the hottest month in Atlanta, this one appeared to be warmer than normal. There were bridesmaids, groomsmen, and ushers. Lita was Poppy's maid of honor, and Jim was an usher. Jim was very stiff, formal, and gentleman-like as he escorted the women down the aisle. Also, my brothers, Larry and Lawrence, served as ushers. That's right, Larry and Lawrence! My brothers had been named after two different celebrities, one named Larry and one named Lawrence. Some of the other ushers included friends and family members. As I looked into the sanctuary I could see that it was quickly filling up.

The second thing I noticed was that the best man was not there: Booker was nowhere to be found. I was getting more than a little concerned, because it was time for the ceremonies to begin. Rather than delaying the ceremonies, I asked my good friend Al Norman if he would stand in as best man. I felt bad about asking Al, especially since I probably should have asked him or George to be the best man in the first place. Al agreed to stand in as best man, and I apologized to him for the last-minute change.

Just as we were ready to march out into the chapel, Booker came running up. To say that I was not happy at Booker's late arrival was an understatement. Anyway, I now had to inform Al that Booker had arrived and that he was going to be the best man after all. I felt bad, but what could I do? I should have left Al as the best man. Booker said he had been out of town and that his flight had arrived late.

The organist had begun playing my cue—and that's when the realization set in: I was soon going to be saying, "I do"! It was now my turn to march down the aisle. I took a deep breath and began walking to the music. I noticed that the chapel was full as I glanced from side to side. I could feel that everyone's eyes were fixed on me. Somehow I made it down the aisle without tripping or losing my step.

I took my place at the altar and waited for Mr. Finley to escort Poppy down the aisle. The organist began playing, "Here Comes The

Bride," and they began marching down the aisle. I looked at Poppy—she was a very beautiful bride! The ceremony was a masterpiece and everyone gave rave reviews!

After the wedding ceremony, most of the guests attended the reception, which was held at the Marriott Hotel in downtown Atlanta in a large indoor atrium area with trees and other foliage. The reception line was set up near the entrance to the atrium. My new wife and I, along with Lita, greeted the guests as they arrived at the reception.

Everything was going well at the reception until we began to run out of hors d'oeuvres. The contract with the Marriott called for unlimited heavy hors d'oeuvres for 200 guests for two hours. There was an obvious delay in replenishment, and the Marriott caterers then began substituting some items I hadn't agreed to use. I asked to speak to the food service manager or the manager in charge of catering the reception. A few minutes later, a man appeared who identified himself as one of the food service supervisors. I asked him why there was a delay in replenishing some items, and why other items were being substituted. He made excuses but could not give me a credible answer. I then asked to see the food service manager, and was told that he was on vacation.

I wanted to be a host, but instead, I had to deal with a food problem. I asked to speak with the hotel's general manager, and after speaking with him, the service improved some, but not to my satisfaction. I felt as if I had been cheated out of nearly five thousand dollars. I decided to deal with the Marriott at a later date, rather than spoil the reception.

After the reception, Jim and Lita chauffeured Poppy and me in their Rolls Corniche. Drivers and pedestrians alike were rubbernecking to see who they probably thought were celebrities in the back seat of the blue and silver Rolls convertible, as Jim drove us to our home in Ellenwood. I was quite surprised that Jim had volunteered to chauffeur Poppy and me in his Rolls. We had another reception at our home in Ellenwood for family and close friends.

We did not begin our honeymoon immediately, but I had planned it, and the itinerary was going to be a surprise for Poppy. We went to New York for a few days, and while we were there Poppy kept asking me where we were going for the honeymoon. She said that she needed to know, so that she would know what to pack. We went shopping on Fifth Avenue, and I kept giving her hints on what type of clothing to buy for the honeymoon, without revealing the destinations. We went to an exclusive luggage and accessories shop on 57th Street, where I purchased two Hartmann suitcases. One of the suitcases was the largest suitcase made by Hartmann. This of course made Poppy even more curious about the honeymoon.

A couple of days before the honeymoon trip began, I showed Poppy the TWA tickets, and was she surprised—we were going on an American Express escorted tour of European countries! The honeymoon itinerary included an initial flight to London's Heathrow Airport and, several days later, a flight from Gatwick to Amsterdam. After spending a couple of days in Amsterdam, we would take a Mercedes coach to Germany, Switzerland, Luxembourg, Belgium, and France—seven countries total.

Poppy and I departed early one afternoon on a non-stop TWA flight to London. My mother had packed us some snacks for the long flight "across the Pond."

* * *

LONDON, ENGLAND

We arrived at Heathrow and took a taxi to our hotel. It was an older hotel, but it was neat and clean. After we got settled in our room, we went down to the lobby and browsed the shops and restaurants. After dinner, we went to the pub in the hotel for a cocktail. I noticed that there were dishes on the bar filled with some type of beans. I asked the bartender about them, and he told me they were coffee beans. Patrons would chew a handful of beans before they left the bar to mask the odor of alcohol. The caffeine would also probably give them a jolt of alertness. I grabbed a handful of beans and threw them in my mouth. I immediately grabbed a napkin and discreetly spat them out. Coffee beans have a horrible taste!

The next day, we met the other members of the tour group. I won't bore you with all of the details of the honeymoon, but I will just give you some highlights of each country we visited. And for the record, the honeymoon was not boring. It was great!

While in London we went to see the play, *Boxing Day*. We visited the expensive department store Harrods. Later that afternoon, we ate at a restaurant in Piccadilly Circus. We toured Buckingham Palace and watched the changing of the guard—and yes, the sentries are hard to distract. The horses were well-groomed and had a silky, shiny finish on their coats. We also saw London Bridge, and it was not falling down!

One day, Poppy and I had lunch on our own in a British pub. I ordered a ham and cheese sandwich and a beer. The beer was so strong it was like drinking a shot of whisky. Businessmen were also having lunch in the pub, and some of them drank at least two beers. When the waitress brought my order, I felt there had been a failure to communicate: she brought me a ham sandwich and a cheese sandwich, and there were no condiments on the bread. No lettuce, tomatoes, or mayonnaise. I sat there puzzled for a second, and then I took the cheese out of one sandwich and put it in the sandwich with the ham. I wondered how to order a ham and cheese sandwich in the same bread?

Our itinerary included approximately two full days in each country. After London, we took a luxury coach (bus) to Gatwick Airport. The trip included travel through some of England's most beautiful country-side.

AMSTERDAM, THE NETHERLANDS

From Gatwick we flew to Amsterdam, where we toured tulip farms with miles and miles of beautiful tulips and occasional windmills. And we drank Heineken beer and ate herring down by the docks. The men at the seaport were dressed in traditional garb. The tour bus also took us by the city's famous red light district, which is really not a red light district any longer because prostitution is now legal in the Netherlands. The next day, we rode to The Peace Palace in The Hague, which is where the World Court is located, known as The International Court of Justice.

BAVARIA, DEUTSCHLAND, GERMANY

Germany was next, and we toured many locations including Frankfort, Wiesbaden, Baden-Baden, Düsseldorf, Cologne, Mannheim, and other cities. We toured the Rhine River and stopped at one of the castles for a guided tour. The countryside along the Rhine was absolutely beautiful with its mountainous terrain with some areas filled with yellow flowering mustard plants and other areas with livestock. It was amazing to see how the cattle and other livestock were able to keep their balance on such an incline (cow-tipping would be very easy). In Wiesbaden, we stayed at the famous Grand Hotel Nassauer Hoff. While there, I went to Casino Wiesbaden. I did not see any slot machines, as you would in the U.S., only roulette tables. I watched the roulette-table players for a while and decided not to play. Everyone was speaking German, and I was afraid that my wager would not meet the floor minimum. The casino was luxurious and obviously catered to the wealthy. Most of the patrons were in formal attire. I felt as if I was in a James Bond movie!

The next day, Poppy and I and some members of the tour group went to an Italian restaurant in Frankfort. The owner spoke German and Italian, but very little English. Some of the tour members had little patience and wanted to leave when they realized that the staff did not speak English. I convinced them to stay, and the restaurant owner and I were somehow able to communicate and determine what everyone wanted to eat. The food was great!

GENEVA, SWITZERLAND

Next, on to Switzerland! As the Mercedes coach was on the way to Geneva, we came upon a scene of policeman conducting an accident investigation. The accident had occurred a few days prior. The coach driver told us that an avalanche had swept some vehicles off the road and down the mountainside. The snow-capped Swiss Alps were beautiful to see but could prove to be dangerous during the spring thaw. As we approached Geneva, we rode alongside Lake Geneva, which had crystal clear water. The Jet d'eau in the lake had a pressure pump system that propelled water approximately 450 feet into the air! The scenery was beautiful, with castles along the mountainside and some sitting at the edge of the lake. We toured a castle that had an actual dungeon where people were tortured in the old days.

The next day, we rode a cable car to a high point of the snow-covered Alps. The ascent to the top of the mountain was silent and serene. Later, we went to a large building in downtown Geneva that had many shops that sold fine watches, jewelry, and other accessories. The building was ten or twelve stories tall and appeared to be a wholesale merchandise mart.

That evening, Poppy and I went to a nightclub in the La Palace Hilton Hotel. This turned out to be a very interesting evening. We were seated next to three beautiful young women who appeared to be of Ethiopian descent. These young ladies tricked me into getting into trouble with Poppy. I noticed that they were talking and giggling as they looked over at our table. Two of them came over to our table and said that it was the other girl's birthday and asked me if I would dance with her to help celebrate. I asked Poppy if she would mind if I danced with the young lady, and she said, "It's okay with me if it's okay with you." I now understand that her response meant no! Anyway, I danced with the birthday girl, and the other two started dancing all around me—in a sensual manner, I might add! I intended to dance only one song, but they kept encouraging me to keep dancing. I was finally able to get away after dancing several songs.

Poppy was not smiling and appeared to be upset. I asked her if she wanted to dance and she gave me the cold shoulder at first, but we eventually danced. While we were dancing, the host seated an attractive young woman next to our table. She had long black hair and appeared to be from a Middle East country. She walked onto the dance floor and started dancing by herself, then she started dancing near me as if I were her dance partner. The other three women came onto the dance floor and started dancing near me as Poppy and I were dancing.

Poppy and I stayed for a little while longer and then decided to leave. I could tell that Poppy was still upset over the incident. Our hotel was only a few blocks away, and we walked back. Poppy began walking fast ahead of me, as if she did not want to walk with me.

I said, "You don't know anything about the streets of Geneva, especially at this hour. I suggest we walk together." Poppy slowed her pace, and we walked back to our hotel together—silently, but together.

The next day, while we were boarding the coach, I noticed that some of the members of the tour group were whispering. Most of the other travelers were senior citizens, and they were all white. One of the older gentlemen looked at me and asked, "Are you a professional baseball player?" Poppy and I looked at each other and smiled. I looked at the gentleman and pleasantly responded, "No, I am not a pro baseball player."

LUXEMBOURG, LUXEMBOURG

The next stop on our itinerary was Luxembourg, a small European country with beautiful scenery and architecture. It has everything from castles to vineyards to rolling hills and a beautiful countryside. We stopped for lunch at a restaurant in downtown Luxembourg, Luxembourg (like New York, New York). We stopped for an hour-long lunch break and it took forty-five minutes for the restaurant to prepare the dish I ordered. It was a fresh fish dish that consisted of five different types of fish. The dish was absolutely delicious, even though I had to consume it in ten minutes.

BRUSSELS, BELGIUM

We soon reached Belgium, which would prove to be the most solemn part of the trip. We stopped at Ardennes American Cemetery in Neuville en Condroz, Belgium. This cemetery contained the remains of World War II servicemen, many from the famous and decisive Battle of the Bulge. More than 5,000 American servicemen are buried at Ardennes beneath row upon row of white crosses. This was only one of the American cemeteries located in Europe. We also toured Bastonge, where the Battle of the Bulge took place. For some reason, I was under the impression that the remains of U.S. serviceman were returned to the States, if at all possible.

The next stop was Brussels, where we stayed for two days, taking in the sights of the city. Brussels has numerous old stone and concrete buildings. Some of the attractions we saw included the Grand Palace, The Royal Palace, and the Galerie Saint Hubert, which is known as the world's first mall and was built in the mid-1800s! We also toured the financial district, where the Bourse, Brussels' stock market, is located. One of the attractions that Brussels is known for is the little boy pee-ing, known as the *Manneken Pis*. Some of the building in Brussels are three hundred-plus years old and were spared during World Wars I and II, when many large cities in Europe were destroyed. Brussels is the European headquarters for many international businesses.

PARIS

The next day we were off to France. We rode through the beauti-ful scenic countryside in our Mercedes coach, stopping at the occa-sional rest area to stretch our legs and use the facilities. While I was standing at a urinal in the men's restroom, a lady walked up to her husband who was standing next to me and asked him for some money. In order to go into the stalls, there was a charge. The lady walked in the men's room like it was no big deal; she got the money and then walked out.

We arrived in Paris in the afternoon and checked in to our hotel. Paris is an exciting city with lots to see and do. We toured the Louvre Museum and saw the Eiffel Tower and the Arc de Triomphe, Notre-Dame Cathedral, the Champs-Elysees, the Arenes de Lutece (a Gallo-Roman amphitheater), and other sights.

On the afternoon that we were touring on our own, Poppy and I missed the coach at the designated pick-up point, due to a misunderstanding. Missing the coach led to an interesting afternoon with a bit of excitement. The coach driver told the group to meet at the theater. Poppy and I were waiting in front of a movie theater, when we should have been waiting in front of a theater in the Louvre theater district. Our hotel was not in downtown Paris, so Poppy and I had to figure out how to get back to the hotel. We felt adventurous and decided to take the subway commuter train—during rush hour. We wrote the name of our hotel on a piece of paper and showed the paper to the ticket agent, but he was busy selling tickets to commuters who were in a hurry to get to their trains. We then showed the paper to commuters who already had their tickets, but most of them were in a hurry to get to their trains as well. Finally, a gentleman who spoke English directed us to the right train and told us where to get off. We purchased our tickets and boarded the train that would leave us near our hotel. The train stopped only a few blocks from our hotel. That evening we went to the world famous Moulin Rouge.

The next day we went to Louis the XIV's Chateau de Fontaine-bleau. The palace and grounds were so large that they could have been considered a city. It was a massive, ornate complex in several sections, one of which was a housing wing for security forces and staff. There were numerous rooms, including bedrooms, parlors, dining halls, ballrooms, and other rooms. The beds were short compared to modern beds because some people during that era slept sitting up. The most impressive room in the palace was the chapel, reminiscent of a small church. This place of solitude allowed a resident to worship, pray, or meditate, without having to go outside.

Well, our fantastic European honeymoon was coming to an end. The next day, we boarded a TWA flight out of Charles De Gaulle International Airport back to Kennedy International. We stayed in New York overnight and the next day returned to Atlanta.

* * *

I returned to my office to find mounds of paperwork waiting to be completed for government contract bids. I continued working long hours during the week and half a day on Saturdays, but no more Sundays.

Coming home in the evening was truly refreshing. The privacy, the quiet, the lake and the trails, the pool, and our house was always refreshing after a hard day at work. Along with the serenity came an occasional surprise. One Saturday afternoon, Poppy and her friend Wanda were planting flowers in a private sitting area off the master bathroom. I kept telling them to keep the door closed to keep out the bugs, mosquitoes, and other critters. Later that evening, Poppy was taking a shower when I heard a loud scream. I ran into the bathroom to see what was wrong. Poppy was standing naked in the shower, pointing to the floor. A small snake was shimmying across the floor. I promptly stunned the snake and then threw it outside. Now came the big question: Where's the mama! Could another snake have gotten into the house? I conducted a thorough search of the house and gave it a clean bill of health. From that day on, no outside doors were left open!

Jim and Lita would occasionally visit with us in Atlanta, and we would sometimes visit with them. One Saturday, Jim and Lita treated us to an outing at Six Flags theme park. Jim's friend and attorney John Taylor accompanied us. While we were walking through the park, Jim spotted a young woman he was familiar with. They made eye contact and acknowledged each other. Jim continued to look at the young lady, even after she had passed by us; he then excused himself and walked back to speak with her. Lita appeared to be very upset as she watched Jim walking over to speak to the woman, but she did not say anything. Jim was gone for approximately a minute. When he returned, Lita looked at him with displeasure, but again, she did not say anything.

A month or so later, Lita came to visit by herself. She was visibly upset and nearly in tears. Lita told Poppy that she was upset because of the way Jim was treating her, and she suspected that he was having an affair. Lita was also upset because Jim had her on a shoestring budget to manage the household and to buy personal items. Amazingly, she was barely able to make ends meet. After becoming frustrated, Lita came to Atlanta and stayed for a couple of days, and then Jim came up and apologized. She then returned home. Jim promised to change or give her more of an allowance. But, unfortunately, this problem arose on more than one occasion. Jim would sometimes buy her an expensive gift to appease her.

∞

CHAPTER 4: THE MARABLES MOVE TO SANDY SPRINGS; THE SULLIVANS MOVE TO PALM BEACH

During the late summer of 1982, the year that Poppy and I got married, we went to the World's Fair in Knoxville, Tennessee. It was a pleasant Saturday in September, not too hot and not too cool. There were lots of exhibits to see and they were spread over a large area, which meant there would be lots of walking. Poppy kept complaining that she was tired, and I figured it was due to all of the walking. After returning to Atlanta, Poppy continued to complain about being tired, and then she missed her monthly cycle. We made an appointment to see Dr. Les Patton, Poppy's OB/GYN. Dr. Patton confirmed our suspicion that Poppy was pregnant!

After the shock wore off, Poppy and I both were very excited about the future addition in our lives. We both called our families and friends and told them the good news.

Things were going well for Poppy and me. We made a pretty good adjustment to marriage. I do think Poppy made a better adjustment than I did. Without sounding chauvinistic, for some reason I believe that women make a better adjustment to marriage. I feel that it is understood by women that family comes first. For some men, getting married does not mean that they stop going out with the guys on Fridays for happy hour. Of course I knew better (most of the time). There were some bumps in the road, but no more than the usual, I'm sure. Poppy also made a good adjustment to being pregnant; she was irritable on occasion, but overall, she did well. We both had very busy schedules and the term of Poppy's pregnancy seemed to pass quickly (for me anyway).

One day during the time of her pregnancy, I got an emergency telephone call at the office regarding Poppy. My office manager interrupted the call I was on and switched me to the person on the other line, who said, "Your wife was in an automobile accident on I-20 at the Glenwood exit ramp. She was taken to Georgia Baptist Hospital. I was driving by and I stopped to see if I could help her."

"Was she seriously injured?" I asked.

"I'm not sure, but the car was damaged pretty bad," he responded.

I immediately left the office and drove to the hospital. I drove like I was still a state trooper headed to a serious personal injury automobile accident. At the emergency room I was directed to the room where Poppy was being examined. The doctor was still examining her when I walked in. Poppy was teary-eyed and obviously shaken. I held her hand and asked her how she was doing. She said that she had not felt the baby move since the accident. I tried to reassure her that the baby was okay, and said that the accident probably scared the baby, just as she was scared. After the examination was completed, the doctor assured us that the baby was fine. Poppy was sore and bruised, but she was otherwise okay. Thank God!

I asked her what happened. She told me that she blacked out while driving and did not remember anything until after she hit the railing on the I-20 overpass. The impact caused substantial damage to the Mercedes, and the insurance company later declared it a total loss.

Poppy made a follow-up appointment with Dr. Patton, who advised her not to drive again until after the baby was born. He also said that Poppy had probably fainted when the accident occurred and emphasized that it could happen again.

Poppy and I decided not to have an ultrasound to determine the gender of the baby, because we wanted to be surprised. However, I was certain that it was going to be a boy, and his name would be Marvin D. Marable II. If by some slim chance it were a girl, her name would be Ingrid Alexandria Marable, partly in memory of Poppy's niece Ingrid, who died after an automobile accident. I was so sure it was going to be a boy, I bought a blue teddy bear for him!

After a couple of false alarms, Poppy was sure it was time for real, and she was right. On June 27th, one week earlier than predicted by the doctor, our son or daughter would be born. I drove Poppy to Georgia Baptist Hospital in Atlanta. Dr. Patton arrived and after a brief examination confirmed that it was time. A few hours later, I witnessed Dr. Patton deliver a beautiful seven-plus pound, nineteen-and-one-half-inch girl! When Dr. Patton said, "It's a girl," I looked at him and asked, "Are you sure?"

He looked at me and said, "Marvin, I've been doing this for over ten years, and I have not made a mistake yet."

A few days later, Poppy and I took our little "Sugar Plum" (as Poppy called her) and "Plum Pie" (as I called her) home. Sometimes, I would call her "Plum Pie Package." One day, my brother Lawrence asked me why I called her "Plum Pie Package." "Because she is a package that was heaven sent!" I replied.

I had been negotiating a contract on a new home in the affluent Powers Lake subdivision, located in the Sandy Springs section of metropolitan Atlanta. Poppy had taken Lita and Jim to see the newly constructed 5,500 square-foot European style stucco home. Later Lita told Poppy that Jim had commented, "If Marvin buys this house, he is a good one." I wasn't quite sure how to take the comment. I guess Jim felt that he was the only one capable of purchasing a luxurious home.

A couple of years earlier, Jim had borrowed money from his company's pension fund and purchased a 13,000 square-foot oceanfront mansion, Casa Eleda, on South Ocean Boulevard in Palm Beach. Jim paid nearly $2 million for the property. Poppy and I would later make several trips to Casa Eleda to visit Lita and Jim. Later, Jim sold the liquor distributorship for $5 million. He then purchased a luxury townhouse in the Buckhead section of Atlanta for nearly $450,000.

One week after Ingrid was born, Poppy and I moved to our new home on Powers Lake Drive. I assured Poppy that the move would be smooth and that she would not have to do anything. How wrong I was! The moving company sent their representative out a few days before the move. He assured me that a large moving truck would arrive at 8:00 a.m. on the day of the move and his men would begin loading the truck. Meanwhile, the packers came out two days before the move and packed all our belongings. Everything was labeled by item, name, and location to be placed in the new house.

On the day of the move, the movers did not arrive until after noon. And instead of providing a large moving truck, they brought a medium-sized truck and had to make two trips. To make a long story short, the move was not completed until two a.m. the next day. Some of the boxes were mislabeled and placed in the wrong rooms. Poppy was supposed to be in the guest bedroom (which was set up first), with Ingrid. Instead, she exhausted herself by arguing with the movers and telling them where to put the boxes.

I did not give the movers the check when they finished unloading the truck. Instead, the next day, I sent a certified letter to the moving company, and copied my attorney. I reached an agreement with the moving company that was mutually satisfactory for both parties.

Our new home was elegant in every respect and possessed every amenity that you could imagine.

After we got settled in the house, we decided to have a party. Lots of friends and some family members attended, and I also invited a few business associates. The party spread all over the first floor. The guests were laughing and talking having a good time. One of the guests was playing the piano in the living room. Lita's sister Valencia and her husband Jeffrey (Jeff) Weiner attended. One young lady that I invited, a business associate, was wearing the same diamond cross necklace that Poppy was wearing. Poppy's had been a gift from me. When I introduced Poppy to the young lady, they both starred at each other's diamond necklace. Merely a coincidence.

Poppy was talking to the wife of one of my doctor friends and asked the doctor's wife when she was due. The young lady did not say anything, but her husband responded, "She's not pregnant, she's just fat; I told her that she needed to lose some weight!" Poppy was apologetic, and the lady appeared to be understanding, but her husband was surely in the doghouse!

When Ingrid was about two years old she was christened at Ebenezer Baptist Church by Dr. Joseph Roberts, the presiding pastor. She was beautiful in her little white dress, hat, and booties. Family members and friends from both sides attended the christening. We had chosen Lita and Jim to be Ingrid's godparents and they were, of course, in attendance.

Things continued to go well for Poppy and me. We had a beautiful little girl who was the joy of our lives. We attended Ebenezer Baptist Church. Business was very good for both of us. Poppy had over four thousand customers with Allstate, and my business was grossing over $1 million a year. Poppy and I both drove new S-class Mercedes. We hired a nanny for Ingrid and we had a housekeeper. A landscaping company maintained the grounds. We even had a milkman delivering milk and other dairy products! At age thirty-four, it seemed that I had it all, including a beautiful wife, a beautiful daughter, a great home in a beautiful neighborhood, nice cars, nice clothing and jewelry; we were financially secure, with investments and money in the bank. We did not want for anything. We vacationed at our place in Hilton Head and wherever else we wanted to go. My business took me to Japan, China, Korea, Hawaii, and throughout the continental United States. Things could not have been any better.

∞

CHAPTER 5: BUSINESS GONE BAD/ MARRIAGES GONE BAD – WIRETAP, SEPARATION, INDICTMENT, AND DIVORCE

Unfortunately, by the end of 1984, things began to change dramatically. Significant government regulatory changes took effect that negatively impacted my business, and by 1985, my business was all but defunct. I began working as a consultant for companies doing business with the federal government.

One day, Poppy told me that Lita and Jim's marriage was on the rocks. She said that Jim had continued to mistreat Lita and that Lita was considering divorcing him. Soon afterward, in August of 1985, Poppy told me that Lita had left Jim in the Palm Beach mansion and filed for divorce in Atlanta. She also said that Lita had rented a U-Haul and hitched it to the back of her Mercedes, then moved into the townhouse in Buckhead. Poppy later told me that Lita had retained Rick Schiffman to represent her, and that Jim had retained his friend John Taylor and another attorney, Jeffrey Bogart.

Lita would frequently come over to our house, and the two women spent a great deal of time together—so much time that I became concerned. I mentioned my concerns to Poppy on several occasions. I told her that she was spending too much time with Lita. I told her that I understood that Lita was her best friend and that she wanted to give her moral support during her divorce, but I was concerned that she would become so sympathetic with Lita during her impending divorce that she would end up getting a divorce as well. My appeals to her seemed to fall on deaf ears. I even had Poppy's sister Yvonne talk with her, but it did not do any good. It was as though Poppy had become a different person, a person I did not know.

Later that year, I sensed that my marriage was beginning to fail. In the latter part of 1985, I discovered a copy of a letter that Poppy had written to an attorney outlining what she wanted in a divorce settlement against me. In order to find out what was going on in Poppy's life, I placed a recording device on my home telephone.

The sole purpose of the device, which I bought at Radio Shack, is to record telephone conversations. The clerk assured me that it was legal to place the device on my telephone and record conversations, but at the time, I did not realize that it was in fact illegal to do so. (The clerk said that if the device were not legal, Radio Shack would not sell it.) I later learned that the device is legal in some states and illegal in others; also, the Supreme Court of Georgia had not made a ruling on such cases. I am not trying to justify my actions, because it was an unethical thing to do, even if it was legal.

For approximately two months I recorded Poppy's and Lita's conversations. Lita would sometimes call the house, and other times she would make calls from our phone. I placed the device on a telephone terminal located in the basement, and concealed it with boxes. Every evening I would get home before Poppy and retrieve the current tape. I listened to the tapes away from the house on a cassette player and stored the tapes in a cassette case, initially hidden in an upstairs bedroom and later in the trunk of my car, and then in an outdoor rented storage unit.

Most of the conversations between Lita and Poppy involved updates on Lita's divorce, their plans to go shopping, plans to go out locally and out of town—and Poppy would discuss divorcing me. Lita was legally separated, and there were a few conversations regarding her dating status.

I contacted John Taylor to discuss possible representation in my divorce suit, which seemed inevitable. I told him about the tapes, and he told me that Jim would be very interested in listening to them. I remember Taylor saying that this was very serious, referring to Lita and Jim's divorce. For some reason, that statement puzzled me for quite a while. What did it mean? I did not retain Taylor to represent me, but I did call Jim to share some information from the tapes with him.

In early February of 1986, I told Jim that I was going to remove the recording device from my telephone. Jim literally begged me to leave the device in place. He agreed to pay me $30,000 if he did not have to pay anything above his postnuptial agreement, which was approximately $250,000. Against my better judgment, I left the device on my telephone.

One evening later in February, I arrived home to find Poppy in the living room playing the piano. I went downstairs to the basement to check the recording device—and it was not there, it had been removed! I walked back upstairs and said, "I believe you have something that belongs to me." Poppy didn't respond; she kept playing the piano. I noticed that her eyes were puffed up and she was crying. I then told her that, at some point, we would need to discuss our divorce.

Later that evening, Poppy and I did talk briefly about getting a divorce. I emphasized that I wanted us to set up an education fund for Ingrid. I told her that I wanted our divorce to be diplomatic and amicable, for Ingrid's sake, if nothing else. I also told her that I did not want to waste a lot of money on attorneys' fees. I emphasized that we could agree on what we wanted without the involvement of attorneys. I also told her that I tried to warn her about spending so much time with Lita. Poppy said that she would think about what we had discussed and she would get back to me in a couple of days.

Several days later, early in the morning, the doorbell rang repeatedly, and there were several loud knocks on the door. I looked out the window to see a Fulton County sheriff's car parked in the driveway. I opened the door and was served with a divorce notice. So much for talking in a few days. I contacted Atlanta attorney Stephen Clifford and retained him to represent me. He advised me not to move out of the house until after the temporary hearing, which would not be scheduled for several weeks, depending on the court docket.

To avoid conflict, I moved into one of the other bedrooms in the house. Thank goodness that the house was large! Obviously, there was a great deal of tension between Poppy and me. I stayed out of town as much as possible to avoid any potential problems. Meanwhile, I leased an apartment in Cobb County. This way, I would be able to move as soon as the temporary hearing was held.

Just before the hearing, I met with Clifford to discuss some details of the impending divorce. I asked him how I should proceed and what I should expect at the hearing. He advised me to make my best offer, and he would submit it to Poppy's attorney before the hearing date. If all went well, a long, dragged-out divorce proceeding could be avoided. Clifford drafted a property settlement agreement and a child support and visitation agreement and sent it to Poppy's attorney, Rick Schiffman. Days before the hearing date, Clifford received a letter from Schiffman, rejecting my proposal.

During the temporary hearing, the judge granted Poppy $200 less per month in child support than I had proposed. The judge granted me temporary visitation on Wednesdays and every other weekend and also set up a holiday and vacation visitation schedule. After the hearing, Poppy was very upset, and asked her attorney not to speak to my attorney while we were all walking down the street.

Later that night, at home in Powers Lake, the tension was at its highest. I walked into the nursery and took Ingrid out of the bed to rock her to sleep. Just as Ingrid fell asleep, Poppy grabbed her out of my arms and said, "Your visitation does not start until this weekend." I did not say anything, and I did not react. I simply walked into another room. Later that evening, Poppy's father stopped by the house. During our conversation he said to me, "I told you when you two got married, if there was any problem, you could send Poppy back to me."

I responded by saying, "The way that she is acting, you can take her right now. I have been trying to act like a respectable gentleman, but Poppy is not acting like a lady." I then went to my bedroom.

The next morning, as soon as Poppy left for work, I called the moving company to come and move my furniture and personal items to my apartment. The house was left in a mess, because I was trying to move my things out before Poppy returned from work. I left a note advising her that I would straighten up the house later.

The next day, I returned to the house to clean up and put things back in order. While I was in the house, I heard the door open. It was Poppy and Lita! I was standing in the family room when they walked into the house. Poppy immediately began yelling at me for removing some items that she claimed belonged to her. She then walked over to a table and picked up a brass-monkey accessory and raised it as if to hit me. Lita yelled out, "Poppy, don't do that!" Poppy continued to advance toward me with the brass monkey raised above her head. I grabbed her wrist and twisted the ornament out of her hand. She had a strong grip, and the twisting motion caused a cut on her hand. I went upstairs and called the Fulton County Police and advised them of the incident and I asked them to send a patrol car out. While I was waiting for the police to arrive, Poppy was following me around the house, wiping the blood from her hand on to my shirt. Shortly afterwards, the police arrived. The officers looked at my shirt, as Poppy walked up with blood all over her hand. I reminded the police that I had called them to report Poppy's behavior. Poppy and I began arguing in front of the police.

The officers were an African-American woman and a white man. The female officer said, "Both of you shut up!" Everyone was startled by the officer's command, including her partner. The female officer then asked me if I had everything I needed from the house and said that if I did, I should leave. Before I left I asked the female officer to advise Poppy that she could have been arrested for assault or attempted assault and battery. The officer advised her, and then I left the house. I had no intention of having Poppy arrested, but I wanted her to know that she could have been.

* * *

Jim wanted to listen to the tapes, and I agreed to mail them to Palm Beach by courier. Jim also wanted to record the tapes, but I objected. Jim agreed that he would listen to the tapes and take notes only. He also agreed to return the tapes directly to me. I then mailed the tapes to him as I had agreed. Later, I traveled to Palm Beach to visit with Jim and to discuss our impending divorces.

Several weeks later, I received a call from Stephen Clifford, who advised me that a package had been delivered to his office, addressed to me. He said that the package came from attorney Jeffrey Bogart's office. I went over to pick up the package, and upon opening it I discovered it was the tapes. But five cassette tapes were missing! I immediately called Bogart's office to question him about the missing tapes. He said that he had received the package from Jim and then sent it to Clifford's office. He said he did not know anything about the missing tapes. I immediately called Jim, who said that he had returned all of the tapes and did not know anything about any missing tapes. I again called Bogart, who repeated that he did not know anything about the tapes. He stated that he hadn't opened the package but had merely sent the package to Clifford. I was furious!

I had previously agreed to testify at Jim's divorce hearings, and a few weeks later I received a subpoena for an upcoming hearing. I did not appear in court for the hearing. As it happened, the hearing was cancelled. I was not subpoenaed to testify in any of Jim's future divorce hearings. I would have no further communication with Jim Sullivan for approximately eight months.

One day I took my car in for routine service. While waiting for a loaner car, I was advised by one of the dealership employees that my wife was at the dealership and that she wanted to get something out of the trunk of my car. I told the employee not to let her get anything out of my car. Apparently, she thought that I had already left the dealership. Poppy, who was accompanied by Lita, was probably looking for the tapes, but I had them in the briefcase that I was holding. Poppy did not get the tapes.

A couple of months later, I learned that the Fulton County District Attorney's office was investigating me for "invasion of privacy" for placing the recording device on my home telephone. I was informed by what I considered a reliable source that the DA's office was going after the downtown lawyers for being involved with the wiretapping of my telephone. I was also informed that the assistant district attorney, who was pursuing the wiretap case, was doing so in an effort to advance his career. As soon as I learned of the investigation, I disposed of the tapes: I took them to Dekalb County one evening, drove to the rear of a shopping center, and threw all the tapes into a dumpster.

Later in the summer of 1986, I was charged with invasion of privacy. I retained attorney Michael Mears, who was able to negotiate an agreement with the DA's office that allowed me to avoid a criminal conviction, and the record was expunged. Contrary to reports in the various media, I have never been convicted of a crime and I do not have a criminal record.

On December 29, 1986, my divorce was finalized, and I was satisfied with the outcome. Poppy and I were divorced exactly ten years after Lita and Jim had gotten married. By now, I had started an airport shuttle service called "Stagecoach" which provided van, bus, and limousine service from the Atlanta Airport to hotels in Vinnings, Cumberland, and other locations in metropolitan Atlanta. I also provided limousine and corporate charter bus services, and continued in my consulting business. When the first of the year came, I wrote in my appointment calendar: "This is going to be a great year!"

On the contrary—it was one of the worst years of my life.

∞

CHAPTER 6: LITA SULLIVAN MURDERED; THE BEGINNING OF THE TWENTY-YEAR CURSE

On January 13, 1987, at 7:02 a.m., I received a voicemail message from Jim Sullivan. I was not at home, but I retrieved the message within minutes of it being recorded. On the recording Jim appeared to be nervous and anxious, which was uncharacteristic of him. The message went as follows: "Marvin, this is Jim. Call me as soon as possible. This is urgent!" I was at a friend's house, and I said to her, "Jim Sullivan called me. I wonder why he's calling me?" As I mentioned before, the last contact that I had had with Jim was in the spring of 1986, more than eight months earlier. I returned the phone call from my friend's home.

Jim wanted to know if I knew if Lita was living at the same address, if she was living alone, and if she still had the same car. I told Jim that I did not know and that I did not have any contact with Lita. I assumed that Jim needed the information to give to a private investigator.

Three days later, on January 16, 1987 at approximately 10:00 a.m., I received a call from my attorney and associate James Booker. I returned the call, but I was not ready for what James was about to tell me.

"James, this is Marvin returning your call."

"Lita has been murdered!" he said. I was in shock and couldn't respond. Before I could collect myself to respond, Booker said, "Poppy and Ingrid were in the house with Lita at the time she was murdered."

"Are they okay? Were they hurt?" I asked. I was frantic!

"I don't know," he said.

I drove home and immediately called Poppy's mother. I asked her if Poppy and Ingrid were okay. She said that they were shaken up, but unharmed. I would have called Poppy, but I did not have her telephone number. She would not have been at home anyway.

I began thinking about the telephone conversation with Jim Sullivan a few days earlier. I immediately assumed that Jim had some involvement in Lita's death. I turned on the television to discover that Lita's murder was the feature story on all of the local networks. There were scenes of the police conducting their investigation in front of the townhouse. The news mentioned that the police were checking for bombs, as the camera showed the police checking out Poppy's Mercedes.

I remembered something that happened earlier that day, as I was about to leave home. An unmarked police car drove by my house with two detectives. At the time I did not pay any attention to their presence and I did not know that Lita had been murdered.

I called my mother and told her what had happened. She was very upset at the tragic news. She extended an invitation for Poppy and Ingrid to come and stay with her in New York, if Poppy wanted to get away from Atlanta for a while. I Informed Poppy's mother of the invitation, but Poppy did not respond. My mother called Al and Cort Norman and gave them the tragic news.

Later that night, after the eleven o'clock news, it began to sink in. Poppy could have been killed and my daughter Ingrid could have been killed. My emotions ranged from sadness to frustration to being angry and then enraged: enraged at Jim Sullivan for doing such a terrible thing by killing Lita or having her killed and for putting my ex-wife and daughter's life in jeopardy. As I thought more and more about what Jim had done, my emotions were trying to take control. At one point, I even contemplated going to Palm Beach and killing Jim. I felt like shooting him in the head with my .357 magnum revolver. Fortunately, being a rational person, the law, consequences, and other factors prevented me from acting on my emotions.

I wanted to reach out to Lita's family and to Poppy, but I was numb and preoccupied with the implications of the early morning telephone call that Jim had made to me on January 13th. I did not attend the memorial service or extend sympathy to the family. For this I apologize.

When I had time to think about what had happened, my investigative mind took over, and I began theorizing about what had happened. I was determined to put all the pieces of the puzzle together. My biggest disadvantage was not having the same information the authorities had. One of my theories was that Jim was attempting to frame me. Jim had convinced me to keep the wiretap on my telephone. Shortly afterwards, Lita and Poppy discovered the device with the assistance of a private investigator. Did Jim somehow tip off Lita or Poppy about the wiretap? What else would have made Lita and Poppy suspect that there was a wiretap on my home telephone? Did Jim then arrange to have Lita killed so the blame could be placed on me, as retaliation? Retaliation for Lita and Poppy giving the wiretap recording device to the district attorney as evidence against me.

Jim supposedly took a private polygraph examination (not administered by the authorities) and passed. One thing seemed certain; Jim was trying to distance himself from Lita's murder. I assumed that the authorities would see right through his deception and stay focused on Jim Sullivan as the prime suspect.

I called Mike Mears and we discussed Lita's murder. Mike advised me not to discuss the case with anyone. Mike and I knew that the authorities would contact me at some point for an interview.

The next time I saw my daughter, I could tell that she was affected by the murder of Lita Sullivan. She seemed nervous and afraid. I am sure that some of this came from the fear that she sensed from her mother. Ingrid would repeatedly say, "Mama Lita was shot, Mama Lita was shot." (Ingrid always called Lita "Mama Lita.") Ingrid had a difficult time going to sleep and when she did she would sleep fitfully, tossing and turning, then waking up crying. I would hold her in my arms and comfort her until she fell back to sleep. I would also kiss her and tell her that I loved her. Lita's murder affected Ingrid for months, if not years. Ingrid was not yet four years old when Lita was killed.

My life would be forever changed by the murder. Every time I went out to social events, people would stare, point, and whisper. Was it paranoia? I don't think so! People would ask me about Lita's murder, and I would tell them that I didn't know anything about the murder. Some people asked me who I thought had killed Lita; others asked me if I thought Jim Sullivan killed her. Again I would say, I don't know.

About two weeks after Lita's murder, I received a voicemail message from the Atlanta Police Department's Homicide Division, asking to set up an appointment to interview me. I called Mike Mears and an appointment was scheduled. We all know how that went, based on the account given in the opening pages of this book. There is one thing I did not know that might have led the authorities to believe I may have been involved in Lita's murder: Mike Mears was one of the top death-penalty defense attorneys in Atlanta, if not the entire Southeast. Did the authorities suspect me more because of his credentials? I suspect they did.

This was the first time that I officially knew I was a prime suspect in Lita's murder. I began feeling humiliated and depressed to think that I, a former law enforcement officer, was being considered a suspect in the most heinous crime I could imagine: murder. The whole situation seemed surreal to me. I was hoping I would wake up one morning and Lita would be alive, and my nightmare would be over. But of course, that did not happen. Instead, I woke up to a perpetual nightmare.

The way the authorities were pursuing their investigation by focusing on me confirmed my theory that Jim was trying to shift the blame towards me by denying his involvement. Although I am sure that the authorities were investigating Jim, I felt that their main focus was on me. As a former law enforcement officer, I kept telling myself that the authorities would have to have some credible evidence to consider me as a suspect. I also knew that Lita's murder would be a death-penalty case, and I assumed that the authorities would be seeking the death penalty. I wanted to help the authorities, but at the same time I felt I had to be cautious and follow the advice of my attorney.

The Atlanta Police Department and other authorities made statements to the media labeling me as a suspect in Lita's murder. I met with Mike Mears and prepared a written statement proclaiming my innocence. In it I said that I had no knowledge or involvement regarding the death of Lita Sullivan. The fact that I suspected Jim was speculative; I had no firm evidence. But I was convinced that he had had Lita murdered. Some lay people do not understand why an innocent person, who is considered a suspect, would refuse to talk with the authorities. But all attorneys clearly understand.

One evening, I was at a restaurant off Piedmont Road, near midtown Atlanta, and Lita's brother Emory McClinton, Jr. was seated nearby with some of his friends. The whispering, pointing, and staring began. Emory then shouted out, "Marvin Marable!" I looked over toward him but I did not say anything. The way that he called out to me was humiliating. The murder investigation made me feel as if I were a dejected outcast; fair game to be stoned.

One day when I picked Ingrid up from daycare, I noticed that she was upset, and she told me that another child in daycare had falsely accused her of doing something. I looked at her and said, "It doesn't feel good when someone accuses you of doing something that you did not do, does it?" She replied in a soft voice, "No daddy, it doesn't feel good." I said, "I know how you feel," as I held her little hand. She then said, "I love you daddy." And I replied, "I love you, too, sweetheart."

∞

CHAPTER 7: JIM SULLIVAN REMARRIES, AND THE INVESTIGATION CONTINUES WITH JIM AND MARVIN AS PRIME SUSPECTS

Eight months after Lita's murder, Jim Sullivan married Hyo-Sook (Suki) Choi Rogers, a woman he had been dating at the time of Lita's death. Jim continued with his Palm Beach lifestyle as if nothing had happened. Media sources in Palm Beach reported that Jim and Suki went out to dinner the evening of Lita's murder. From what I learned from friends and associates Jim did not send the McClintons a sympathy card or call them. Of course he could have been advised by his attorneys not to have any contact with the McClintons. It appeared that, far from being in mourning, Jim was celebrating.

The investigation continued, but the Atlanta Police did not seem to be making any progress. Eventually, the GBI and the FBI joined them in the investigation of Lita Sullivan's murder. A reward was offered for information leading to an arrest and conviction in the case, but it did not bring forth any credible information. The authorities stepped up their investigation by contacting my friends, acquaintances, and business associates. I received telephone calls from friends and associates all over the United States, telling me that the FBI had called them regarding a murder investigation in Atlanta that involved me. The FBI's investigation had a negative impact on my consulting business. The authorities even contacted my former law enforcement employers and an FBI friend of mine.

I am certain that I was being followed by the FBI and that my telephone was bugged. Having previously worked in law enforcement and having followed people, I would sometimes pick out the authorities as they sat in their vehicles and as they followed me on the road. Paranoia? I don't think so!

One day I received a call from attorney James Booker suggesting we have dinner. Booker was in the process of getting a divorce from his wife, Iva. Booker was someone I had considered a friend, but our friendship was not as close as it had been in the past.

We met at a restaurant near Cumberland Mall. I thought Booker began acting a little peculiar as soon as he arrived. He stated my name loud and clear. He also made mention of the time and the name of the restaurant. His demeanor seemed official, not casual. I asked him how his divorce was coming and how his two small sons were, and he said that he was still in the process of divorcing Iva and that he had not seen his boys for nearly a year. He tried to offer some rational reason for not seeing his sons, but I intervened and said, "You need to see your children. How could you not want to see your kids?" Booker sounded as if he were avoiding seeing his sons to spite his wife.

Booker then began talking about his divorce and how he was not happy with the way it was proceeding. While James was talking, it almost appeared as if he were in the middle of a deposition. This behavior was uncharacteristic of Booker; he did not seem like the same person who had been the best man at my wedding, who owned real estate with me in Hilton Head, and who purchased my mini-ranch in Ellenwood.

Booker then asked me a question that all but confirmed that he was wearing a wire, one that shocked me: "If someone wanted to get rid of someone, how would they go about doing it?"

After a pause, I replied, "I don't know how you or anyone else would go about getting rid of someone." I then advised Booker that if he was thinking about doing something illegal, he should get the thought out of his head; at which point he excused himself to go to the lavatory. When he returned from the lavatory he did not ask me any more questions of that kind. If I suspected that Booker was about to harm Iva, I would have reported him to the authorities, but I was convinced that there were other motivations.

I would later learn that James Booker was under investigation by the IRS for possible money laundering and income-tax evasion. Is it possible that he was trying to implicate me in Lita's murder in exchange for a deal with the IRS or other authorities? I began to distrust Booker and some of my other so-called friends and associates. I stopped going to most social events and became something of a recluse.

One day, I returned home to find a voicemail message from Jim. "Marvin, this is Jim. Give me a call." Of course I did not return his call, but I did inform Mike Mears of the call.

The authorities were having a difficult time trying to solve the murder of Lita Sullivan. They continued to focus on me as one of the prime suspects. Unfortunately, when the authorities label someone a suspect (especially in a high-profile case), the public has a tendency to assume that that suspect is guilty. Even though one is supposedly presumed innocent until proven guilty, I felt as if I were already convicted and waiting to be sentenced. My greatest fear became being falsely charged and convicted of Lita's murder, and in a capital murder case, falsely executed. It has happened in the past and it could happen in the future.

∞

CHAPTER 8: THE FEDERAL INVESTIGATION

One day, while I was at home watching television, my doorbell rang. I was not expecting anyone. I looked through the peephole and saw a woman in business attire, alone. Perhaps a reporter? I thought.

"Who is it?"

"FBI," she responded.

Would they send a lone female FBI agent to arrest me, I asked myself? Maybe the cavalry is standing off to the side in an effort to avoid a possible altercation. Is this their strategy? Enough self-questions and possible reasons for the FBI being at my door. I opened the door and learned the real reason. The agent introduced herself as she showed me her identification. She appeared to be in her mid-thirties and had a pleasant personality. She was also nice looking, I might add. I invited her in.

Would the cavalry now come charging in? I noticed papers in her hand as I offered her a seat. Possible search warrant? Hardly; that would bring an army of agents. Before she sat down, and during her time in the house, she was inconspicuously but methodically looking around, as if she were taking a mental picture of everything. She then informed me that I had been subpoenaed to testify in a federal grand jury investigation regarding the murder of Lita Sullivan. She then handed me the subpoena and asked me if I had any questions, and I said, "No."

After the agent left, I read the subpoena. I was listed as a target of the investigation, and as a "putative defendant." I called Mike Mears, who again advised me not to make any statements or give any testimony to the authorities or the grand jury. Mears drafted a letter for me to give to the assistant United States attorney which asserted my Fifth Amendment rights against self-incrimination.

I appeared in front of the grand jury the next week at the Richard B. Russell Federal Building, and I gave the letter to Assistant United States Attorney William McKinnon. Detective Welcome Harris was visibly disturbed and began to sigh in disappointment as the letter was read. I then left the building.

I called Mears and told him that I had refused to testify, as he had instructed. Mike advised me that the U.S. Attorney's Office would not subpoena me to testify in front of a federal grand jury, if they had had enough evidence to indict me. I told him that I would be glad when Lita's murder was solved, so that I could clear my name and get on with my life.

My family became increasingly concerned about the investigation as the authorities' attempted to build a case against me for the murder of Lita Sullivan. My mother, in particular, was very disturbed by the investigation and its implications. I later learned from my Aunt Priscilla (Sis) that my mother would often call her and begin crying because of her concern for me. My aunt also told me that a network of family members and friends had an independent nationwide prayer vigil for me every day at noon. My mother also asked me to read a passage from the Bible every day. It was Psalm 91, which reads as follows:

"He that dwelleth in the secret place of the most high shall abide under the shadow of the Almighty.
I will say of the Lord, he is my refuge and fortress: my God; in him will I trust.

Surely he shall deliver thee from the snare of the fowler, and from noisome pestilence.

He shall cover thee with his feathers, and under his wings shalt thou trust: his trust shall be thy shield and buckler.

Thou shalt not be afraid for the terror by night; nor the arrow that flieth by day;

Nor for the pestilence that walketh in darkness; nor for the destruction that wasteth at noonday.

A thousand shall fall at thy side, and ten thousand at thy right hand; but it shall not come nigh thee.

Only with thine eyes shalt thou behold and see the reward of the wicked.

Because thou hast made the Lord, which is my refuge, even the most high, thy habitation;

There shall be no evil befall thee, neither shall any plague come nigh thy dwelling.

For he shall give his angels charge over thee, to keep thee in all thy ways.

They shall bear thee up in their hands, lest thou dash thy foot against a stone.

Thou shalt tread upon the lion and adder: the young lion and the dragon shalt thou trample under foot.

Because he hath set his love upon me, therefore will I deliver him: I will set him on high, because he hath known my name.

He shall call upon me, and I will answer him: I will be with him in trouble; I will deliver him and honour him.

With long life will I satisfy him, and show him my salvation."

After I had read the psalm a number of times, the meaning became crystal clear to me, based on my interpretation. No matter how powerful and mighty you think you are (the authorities), and no matter what your intentions are, there is a power that is greater and mightier than you are. And you will not be able to touch me, because I am being shielded by this power that is mightier than you. I read this psalm nearly every day for almost two years.

The media made me out to be some type of mysterious individual who associated with known criminals who had been in and out of jail for most of their lives. On September 16, 1991 the Atlanta *Journal-Constitution* (AJC) published an article that read: "A confidential inform-ant (Johnny Austin Turner) told Mr. Letcher that he (Henley) and another man were involved in the murder. According to the affidavit, investigators believe the man is Marvin D. Marable." Another article published by the AJC the next day read: "According to the affidavit, investigators identified the man as Marvin D. Marable, a New York native." The Marietta *Daily Journal* published an article on September 17, 1991 which read: "Henley, Botts, Marable and Sullivan are listed in the affidavit as suspects." There were similar articles published in other media.

After the media portrays you as a villain, it is extremely difficult to remove the label. The media uses statements such as, "We attempted to contact John Doe, but he refused to comment," or "He was not available for comment." Negative comments by the media make it appear as if the person under suspicion or implicated in an investiga-tion, is actually guilty. I have never heard the media make the follow-ing statement: "John Doe has been advised by his attorney to refrain from speaking to the media, because any statement that he makes might be misinterpreted and lead to a false assumption or conclusion." The media also rarely issues retractions after condemning an inno-cent person. Unfortunately, when the media or the authorities state that you are a suspect, the public often assumes you are guilty. And it would be extremely unfortunate if a judge or jury also assumed that you were guilty.

* * *

MARVIN MARABLE MOVES TO NEW YORK

I decided to dissolve the airport shuttle service and move back to New York. In the spring of 1990, I moved to Mount Vernon. Most of the people that I knew in New York (outside of my family) were unaware of Lita's murder and the fact that I was considered a suspect. The whole situation still seemed surreal to me, even though I knew it was very real. When I read my name in the newspaper, it was as if I were reading about someone else, not me. I kept hoping I would wake up from the nightmare and it would be over, but that did not happen. It would last for nearly twenty years.

In the back of my mind was the fear that the authorities would one day ring the doorbell and arrest me for Lita's murder, even though I had absolutely nothing to do with it.

Early one morning I was awakened by the sound of several vehicles pulling up and stopping in front of the house. I then heard doors slamming, and looked out of the window to see eight plainclothes officers getting out of the vehicles. I said to myself, "Well, I guess this is it." To my surprise however, the officers walked across the street to the Bennetts' residence. The authorities were looking for Michael Bennett, who was wanted on an outstanding "failure to appear" warrant relating to a larceny charge. When the authorities were told that Michael was not at home, they got back in their vehicles and drove off.

There was someone outside of my family that I could trust, who would not make me feel as if I were being interrogated: my former fiancée, Renee Guy, the same Renee who threatened to come to Chicago at an awkward moment, as mentioned earlier in the book.

Renee and I had dated for several years before I moved from New York to Chicago. I am still not quite sure how to explain what happened between Renee and me, but at some point our relationship became strained, and Renee seemed to lose interest. Years earlier, Renee and I were living together, and one evening I returned home to find an out-of-state application for graduate school. Earlier, we both had decided to go to graduate schools in the same area. Renee was going to pursue a degree in public administration, and I was going to go to law school. We had discussed going to graduate schools, but only in New York State.

When Renee came home, I asked her about the application. She became defensive and said that she didn't want to limit her options to New York. A few days later, I found the engagement ring I had given her, placed in my jewelry box. I did not question her about returning the ring. I took it to mean that the engagement was off. Being in denial, I left the ring in my jewelry box for a few days, hoping that she would take it back. During this time, I was still employed with the New York State Police. I had built a home upstate on several acres in Columbia County, New York, in the town of Livingston. The property sat on a hilltop and offered beautiful views of the Berkshire Mountains and the Hudson River Valley. The upstate county was unique because it provided views of Connecticut, Massachusetts and Vermont. I could even see the mountaintop that was central to the legend of Rip Van Winkle. I sometimes crossed the Rip Van Winkle Bridge to get to my house.

I moved my belongings out of Renee's apartment one day while she was at work. Later that evening, I received a call from my friend Al Norman, asking me what I had done to Renee. Renee had called him crying and upset because I had moved out. As I said earlier, I am not sure what happened to Renee and me.

* * *

I knew that Renee was currently working for the County of Westchester, and I decided to give her a call. I called her at work— and I took a deep breath when the phone began to ring. After a couple of rings, I heard, "Renee Guy."

"Hello Renee, this is Marvin."

"MARABELL!" she replied. As I mentioned earlier, most New Yorkers pronounced my last name as "Mara-bell," and some close friends called my brothers and me, "Bell." Renee was happy to hear from me, and she was aware of what was going on in Atlanta. We made plans to meet on the upcoming weekend.

On Saturday, I drove to Hartsdale. Renee lived in a secluded area off a side street in a very private area of Hartsdale, with very little car traffic. Renee asked me if I wanted to go to see the Sculpture Gardens at PepsiCo's headquarters in Purchase, New York. It sounded like a good idea, so we drove to Purchase. On the way there, we mainly engaged in small talk.

We arrived at PepsiCo early in the afternoon. It was a nice clear day with a slight chill in the air; after all, it was springtime in New York. We began walking slowly along the pathway looking at the sculptures and the wildlife. As we walked along the lake, Renee turned and looked at me and asked, "Marvin, how are you doing?" I knew it was going to be a serious question when she started off by saying my first name.

I replied, "I've been better." Renee never asked any specific questions regarding the investigation of Lita's murder. She was only concerned about my well-being. Renee was so friendly, warm, and comforting, it was as if we had never stopped dating, and as if we were still engaged to be married. It reminded me of when Renee and I and Al and Cort would hang out together. I remember one holiday—possibly the Fourth of July—the four of us spent the day at Lake Taghkanic State Park, not far from my house in Livingston. Al and I had rented a canoe, and we were attempting to row it back across the lake where the ladies were. Al and I did not know what we were doing and we kept rowing around in circles. We tried to play it off as if we knew what we were doing and that we wanted to go in circles. We could not fool the ladies, but by the time they got in the canoe, we rowed like pros! I missed those times.

I began telling Renee what I had been going through for the past few years. Renee interrupted me and said that I did not have to talk about it, and that she was just concerned about my well being. I told her that it was ok and I continued. I told her how the past few years had been extremely difficult with the false allegations, the news media and other media sources all but destroying my credibility, and I told her how much it hurt. I continued by telling her that I could not defend myself and refute the allegations because my attorney advised me not to talk to the authorities. I reminded Renee of the disparity in the criminal justice system when it came to African-Americans. I told her what happened as soon as I arrived at the Atlanta Police Department for an interview after Lita's murder. I went on to tell her about the early morning desperate telephone call that Jim Sullivan made to me on January 13th. I told Renee that I was certain that the authorities would be seeking the death penalty for Lita's murder.

I continued to pour my heart out to Renee as we held hands and walked through the gardens, looking at the beautiful sculptures. Renee listened without interrupting me or questioning me. We would occasionally stop and take photographs of each other and the sculptures. We spent several hours there, then we went to get something to eat. Renee said that she was happy I was back in New York. I told her I did not know how long I would be in New York (referring to the authorities possibly falsely charging me for Lita's murder). After dinner, we returned to Renee's home and talked until it was very late. It felt as if we caught up on everything that had transpired in our lives since we separated.

While driving back home to Mount Vernon, I began thinking about the investigation in Atlanta and feeling that I would be arrested and charged as being an accomplice or conspirator in Lita's murder. Whenever I was alone, my mind would automatically default to thinking about the murder investigation. Whenever I was with family or friends, I welcomed the diversion from the investigation.

After spending several weeks in New York, I decided to take a much-deserved vacation. The next day, I booked a flight to Jamaica out of Newark International. A week later, I was on my way to sunny Jamaica.

Just as I was about to board my flight, the strangest thing happened. I was walking down the jetway when two U.S. Customs agents, a man and a woman, stopped me. I didn't see them until I was far into the jetway. The female agent showed me her identification then asked to see mine. As I showed her my ID, she began asking me questions—and you can imagine what was going through my mind. I thought I was going to be arrested while boarding the airplane. She asked me if my trip was business or pleasure. I told her it was pleasure. She wanted to know how long I planned to stay in Jamaica and I said, five days. She wanted to know where I would be staying. I told her the Wyndham Hotel in Rose Hall. She then asked me if I was carrying more than ten thousand dollars in cash or other funds. I told her no. She then handed my identification back to me and said, "Mr. Marable, enjoy your vacation."

I entered the airplane and felt as if my vacation was ruined before it even began. Was I being paranoid, or did those questions have something to do with the investigation? If the authorities had my telephone bugged in New York, they would have known I booked a trip to Jamaica. Was this an attempt to intimidate me? I made up my mind right then that nothing was going to spoil my vacation!

I arrived at the airport in Montego Bay early in the afternoon. As soon as I stepped off the plane, I felt the tropical humidity and the intense heat of a beautiful sunny afternoon. After I cleared customs (without incident), I took a cab to the hotel, where I was greeted by the bellman as soon as I stepped out of the taxi. As I walked to the registration counter, I convinced myself that I was not going to think about the investigation, and I was going to have a great time.

I checked in and went to my oceanfront room. I walked over to the window and looked out at the beautiful Caribbean. After I unpacked, I decided to go to the guest "welcome orientation." The guest-services manager, who introduced herself as Heather Jones, proceeded to tell the new guests the dos and don'ts that would ensure we enjoyed our stay. Ms. Jones was a very attractive woman, and seemed very professional. After the orientation, I changed and headed for the beach. On my way, I walked through the hotel lobby and saw Heather sitting at her desk. I walked over to her and introduced myself. "My name is Marvin Marable, Ms. Heather Jones."

She appeared to be busy, but she politely replied, "Hello, Mr. Marable."

"You can call me Marvin," I responded. "I see that you are busy, so I won't keep you from your work." She smiled, and I said, "I'll see you later." I then walked out to the beach.

The sun was shining brightly and the soft tropical breeze was refreshing. Vacationers were swimming, walking in the sand, and sitting in beach chairs enjoying tropical drinks with little umbrellas in them. I swam for a while, then lounged in a beach chair for a couple of hours before heading back to my room. On the way to my room, I walked though the hotel lobby and stopped by to see Ms. Jones. She was still busy at work, so I just smiled and said hello.

For the next few days, I did the usual touristy things, such as going on tours, visiting the local shops, and visiting the spirit of the "White Witch" at the Great House of Rose Hall. Folk tale has it that Annie Palmer, the "White Witch," was known as the mistress of voodoo. Palmer's husband supposedly died suspiciously. It was also said that in the 1800s Palmer would either lure or command slaves to her bedroom at night, and subsequently kill them. Palmer was said to have been killed by slaves in the slave uprising in the 1830s. I also participated in some of the events hosted by the hotel. I met some nice people, mainly from the States. In the evening, I would sometimes visit the hotel nightclub. I was on a "golf package," and that's about the only thing I did not do. I didn't feel like playing golf! I continued to stop by and speak to Heather at least once during the day. I would talk with her for a while if she was not busy.

Before I knew it, my vacation was coming to an end. Before I left the hotel, I stopped by to say goodbye to Heather. I gave her my telephone number and address and asked her to call me if she ever came to New York. She was a very pleasant person, and I felt as if we had become friends in the short period of time we spent together. She said she would call me if she came to New York, but I didn't really think she would call me or that I would see her again. I figured that she met a lot of single guys at the hotel and that I was just another guy.

Later I boarded the plane back to the States. The vacation had been a welcome diversion, but as the plane was preparing to land, I began thinking about the investigation.

Renee and I would talk on the telephone and occasionally see each other, and sometimes we would go out together. One weekend, we went to the Caramoor Arts Festival in Katonah, New York. Renee was able to focus on our relationship, but it was extremely difficult for me to reciprocate. It seemed as if I was always preoccupied, or even obsessed with the investigation.

I decided to go to graduate school and possibly on to law school. But first I enrolled in the State University of New York (SUNY) at Purchase to take a writing course and a computer course to get me ready for grad school. I also secured full-time employment in corporate security with Bayer AG, a Fortune 200 company, and I continued my government contract consulting business. I had to establish new business relationships, since the authorities had all but ruined my existing relationships. The preoccupation with work, the consulting business, and the college courses helped to distract me from the investigation.

Renee and I began seeing each other less often; not because of her, but because of me. I enjoyed being with her, but I could not seem to activate my feelings; it's as if they were numb. I certainly did not want to hurt us again. Our relationship seemed to fade away. I guess the timing was bad. I would occasionally go out, but I was not looking to cultivate a new relationship.

Several months later, I received an unexpected phone call. "May I speak with Marvin Marable?" a woman asked.

"This is Marvin," I replied in a puzzled voice.

"This is Heather," she said. I was asking myself who Heather was, but before I could say anything, she said, "Heather Jones from the Wyndham Rose Hall in Jamaica."

"Oh, Heather! How are you doing?"

"I'm doing fine. I'm visiting a friend in Queens," she replied.

"How long are you going to be in New York?" I asked.

"For about a month or two."

"We will have to get together while you're here," I said.

"My birthday is next week," she said.

I asked her if she had any plans, and she said that she and her friend Andrea were planning to go to a nightclub in Manhattan on Saturday to celebrate her birthday. She told me that I was welcome to join them, and I accepted the invitation. Heather gave me the telephone number and the address where she was staying in Queens, and I said I would see her on Saturday at 9:00. "What a pleasant surprise," I said to myself. I had not expected to hear from her. And I figured it would be okay to go out with Heather, because I did not feel as if she would be pursuing a relationship. Besides, she was only going to be in the U.S. for a couple of months at most.

On Saturday evening, the three of us went to a nightclub on the Lower East Side called the Pulse. The DJ played mainly reggae music.

Both Heather and Andrea were very attractive in their mini-dresses. We danced and talked and we had a very good time. I drove them back to Queens, and I told Heather that I enjoyed myself and I hoped to see her again soon. She said she would like that.

As I was driving back to Mount Vernon, I said to myself, "What if she knew about the investigation?" She would probably be afraid to talk to me. I had told her that I was divorced and that I had a daughter; that was the extent of what I said about Atlanta and my life there. I reminded myself again that she would only be here temporarily, and that the situation in Atlanta would not matter.

Heather and I went out several more times during the next couple of months. She said she had to return to Jamaica and take care of some business, and afterwards, she would be returning to Queens.

One day, I received a call from Mike Mears. Before he could say anything beyond "Hello," I said, "Mike, I hope that you're calling about the bill." (As opposed to something worse.)

Mike laughed and said, "No, I'm not calling about the bill." He advised me that he had received a call from the U.S. Attorney's Office, and they were offering me immunity in exchange for truthful testimony. I said that I was not interested in being granted immunity. Mike clarified that I was being granted "use" immunity, which is forced immunity. He told me that if I did not cooperate and testify, I could be cited for contempt and even put in jail indefinitely. I told Mike that although I had not been charged with Lita's murder I did not want it to appear as though I were striking a deal with the authorities for a lighter sentence. In my opinion, whenever the public hears the word "immunity," they usually assume that the person is guilty and that they have struck some kind of deal. Immunity usually involves testifying against a codefendant in exchange for a lighter sentence, such as avoiding the death penalty in a murder case.

Even though I did not like the idea of immunity, Mike and I agreed that it was a mixed blessing. Good, because I would have a chance to set the record straight with the authorities, if no one else; bad, because to the public, it would seem as if I agreed to cooperate for a lighter sentence. One thing was for certain: I could not now be falsely convicted of Lita's murder, sentenced to death, and executed. The immunity was also an assurance that I would not even be falsely convicted and serve any prison time. So the good outweighed the bad.

Heather returned to New York from Jamaica, and I figured it was a good time to tell her what had happened in Atlanta and what was going on regarding the case. I also explained "use" immunity, and how I felt I was being forced to testify. She was of course surprised to hear all this, but she was mainly concerned about how I was dealing with the situation.

Several days later, I flew to Atlanta out of LaGuardia. When I arrived, I rented a car and drove to the after-school daycare to surprise my daughter. I walked in and showed my identification to the attendant. I then heard Ingrid scream, "Daddy!" as she came running towards me with open arms. I picked her up, embraced her, and gave her a big hug and kiss. She held my neck so tight that it almost cut off my circulation. Ingrid gave me a big smile that showed a front upper tooth missing. Ingrid was seven years old by now, and she attended Eastside Christian School. She was wearing the blue, burgundy, and gray plaid school uniform. Although I spoke with Ingrid once or twice a week on the telephone, I had not seen her for several months, and it was great seeing her. I truly missed seeing her regularly, just as I did when I lived in Atlanta. I took her out to dinner and she brought me up to date on everything that was going on in her life. After we finished eating, I drove her home and gave her another big hug and kiss. I told her that I loved her, and that I would see her before I returned to New York.

I met with Mike Mears the next morning. The U.S. Attorney's office and other law enforcement officials wanted to meet with me before I testified in front of the federal grand jury. Mike and I talked briefly before we entered the Richard B. Russell Federal Building. We then checked in at the main reception area, and were escorted to a conference room. When we entered, there were five law enforcement officials present from the U.S. Attorney's Office, the FBI, the GBI, and the Atlanta Police Department. Present were William L. McKinnon and

Robert F. Schroeder from the U.S. Attorney's Office; Todd P. Letcher, special agent with the FBI; Robert F. Ingram, special agent with the GBI; and Detective Welcome Harris from the Atlanta Police Department. I sat at the end of the conference table with my back to the door, Mears sat to my right. Assistant U.S. Attorney McKinnon introduced himself and the other law enforcement officials. I remembered Detective Harris from the Atlanta Police Department.

McKinnon handed Mears a copy of the use immunity agreement. After reviewing it, Mike reviewed it with me. I then signed the agreement and was given a copy.

Assistant U.S. Attorney Schroeder began the questioning.

"Mr. Marable, I want you to tell us everything that you know about the murder of Lita Sullivan." He asked this in an accusing tone.

I looked directly at him and said, "I do not know anything about the murder of Lita Sullivan!"

"Don't tell me that you do not know anything about Lita Sullivan's murder," Schroeder said, while raising his voice.

"I told you that I do not know anything about Lita's murder."

Schroeder was about to respond, when Mears interrupted and said, "Excuse us for a moment." Mike and I then stepped outside of the conference room. Mike said, "Try not to get upset. They obviously think you were somehow involved with Lita's murder. Just tell them what you do know." Mike and I then returned to the conference room. Mike advised the authorities that while I did not have any knowledge regarding Lita's murder, I would tell them what I knew about James Sullivan.

I said, "Before I begin, there is something I would like to say. For nearly five years, you people have been investigating me regarding Lita Sullivan's murder. You interfered with my personal life, my social life, and with my business clients. You have contacted people and informed them that you were investigating me regarding a murder. You have also contacted my former law enforcement employers. You have all but ruined my life, and I want to know why. Why do you think I had something to do with Lita's murder?" They all looked at each other without commenting. I then said, "Now I will tell you what I do know.

I had not seen or spoken with Jim Sullivan since the spring of 1986, because of a dispute involving the tapes."

One of the assistant U.S. attorneys asked, "What kind of dispute?" I said that Sullivan did not return all of the tapes to me as he had agreed. He then asked, "Where are the tapes?" I informed him that I had disposed of them in a dumpster in back of a shopping center in Dekalb County. I then said, "After eight months of no contact with Jim Sullivan, all of a sudden, he calls me early one morning. He called me just after 7:00 a.m., on January 13th, 1987. I was staying at a friend's house the night before, so Jim left a message on my voicemail."

One of the investigators asked, "Who did you stay with that night?"

"I stayed with a friend named Stephany Davis." I then gave them Stephany's telephone number and address, as they requested. Then I continued, "I called home from Stephany's house to retrieve my messages. Jim seemed to be nervous and anxious, which is very uncharacteristic of him. He said, 'Marvin, this is Jim, it is important that I speak with you as soon as possible, it's urgent!' I looked at Stephany and said, 'Jim Sullivan just called me. I wonder what he wants? He said that it was urgent that he speaks to me as soon as possible.' Stephany replied, 'Call him and see what he wants.'"

"I called Jim, and he immediately began asking me questions. 'I need some information. Do you know if Lita is still living in the townhouse? Is anyone living with her? Is she still driving the same car?' He asked the questions in rapid succession, almost without pausing. I responded, 'I don't know. I do not have any contact with Lita. My divorce was finalized at the end of December.' He then said, 'If you find anything out, let me know; this is very important.' I repeated, 'Jim, I do not have any contact with Lita.' He then replied, 'Well, if you find out anything, let me know as soon as possible.' He then hung up the phone. I was very puzzled. Stephany asked me what Jim wanted. I told her that he wanted information on Lita."

One of the investigators asked, "Did Jim Sullivan tell you why he needed the information?"

"No," I replied.

The investigator then asked, "Did you ask him?"

"No, I assumed he needed the information to give to a private investigator."

FBI agent Todd Letcher asked me how I found out about Lita's murder. I said that I'd received a call from attorney James Booker. They all looked at each other but did not say anything.

"Why did you refuse to cooperate with the Atlanta Police Department, and not share this important information?" Letcher asked.

I looked at Detective Harris when I replied, "I was considered a suspect from the beginning. When I went to the Atlanta Police Department for what I thought would be an interview, the first thing that Detective Harris did was to read me my rights." The agents and the assistant U.S. attorneys looked at Harris, but they did not say anything.

The questioning continued. "Have you ever been to the Howard Johnson Motel on Roswell Road?"

"My airport shuttle service has picked up and dropped off customers at the Howard Johnson Motel on Roswell Road," I said.

"Have you ever stayed overnight at the Howard Johnson Motel on Roswell Road?"

"No, I have not."

"Do you know any of the following individuals: Thomas Bruce Henley, Clinton Botts, or Johnny Austin Turner?"

"No, I do not."

"Have you ever been in the Jolly Fox Lounge on Stewart Avenue?"

"No, I have not," I responded.

"Do you know anyone that goes by the name Johnny Furr?"

"No, I do not."

"Mr. Marable, when was the last time that you saw Mr. Sullivan?"

"The last time I saw Jim Sullivan was in the spring of 1986."

"When was the last time you spoke with Mr. Sullivan?"

"The last time I spoke with Mr. Sullivan was the morning of January 13th, 1987. He did call me one time after that date, and left a voice message, but I did not return his call."

"Did you go to see James Sullivan in Palm Beach?" one of the investigators asked.

"Yes."

The investigator continued his questioning by asking; "When did you go and how did you get there?"

"I flew down on Delta Airlines around March or April of 1986." After I responded, the authorities were looking at their notes as if they were puzzled. When I flew down to Palm Beach, I hadn't used my name, I'd used a fictitious name. I told them that I flew down to Palm Beach using the name John Smith.

The questioning continued for about another forty-five minutes or so. At the end of the session, agent Letcher asked, "Mr. Marable, would you be willing to submit to a polygraph examination?"

I looked at Mike Mears. Mike said, "As long as the polygraph interview is covered under the immunity agreement, I have no objection." Agent Letcher and the assistant U.S. attorneys conferred, and agreed that it would be covered.

I then said, "Yes."

Agent Letcher said that he would make the call and set up the interview for the next day. He and I then spoke briefly and he gave me information about the polygraph examination. He then asked me, "Why don't you get back into law enforcement?"

"Would the FBI hire me?" I asked.

Letcher just looked at me, but did not respond.

Mike Mears and I then went to a waiting room next to the grand jury room. Mike said that he felt the interview had gone well.

"I felt as if a heavy weight had been lifted off my chest," I said. I then added, "The U.S. attorneys and the FBI seemed shocked when I told them that the Atlanta Police read me my Miranda rights as soon as I arrived for the interview." Mike agreed with me.

For some reason, I did not trust the authorities, and I felt that they still considered me a suspect. Mike and I wondered why they were asking me questions about people I did not know and about a place I had not been. What was the connection? As a former investigator, I was not accustomed to being kept out of the loop. It was frustrating and led to a lot of speculation, which is what you have to deal with when you do not have facts.

Mike advised me that while he could not accompany me into the grand jury room, if I had any questions during the proceeding, I could ask to speak with him. Just as Mike finished talking with me, a man walked up to me and asked, "Are you Marvin Marable?"

Mike and I looked at each other, and I said, "Yes, I am."

The man showed me his identification and said, "I am a special agent with the IRS."

"What now?" I asked.

The IRS agent told me that I was not the target of his investigation. I said to myself, "Thank goodness. I could not afford to be a target of another investigation."

He said, "Mr. Marable, I would like to ask you some questions regarding some real estate transactions involving you and Mr. James Booker, specifically on Hilton Head, South Carolina and in Ellenwood, Georgia." He wanted specific information pertaining to the percentage of ownership and the dollar amount of the transactions. I gave him the information and he thanked me. I then asked him what this was pertaining to, but he said that there was an ongoing investigation and that he could not tell me any more than that. The agent then asked for my address and telephone number and said that I might be subpoenaed to testify regarding the investigation of James Booker. Just as he was leaving, I was called to testify in front of the grand jury regarding Lita Sullivan's murder.

Assistant U.S. Attorney Schroeder was going to be asking the questions. After I was sworn in, Schroeder began asking me questions regarding my so-called relationship with James Sullivan. He then asked detailed questions regarding the telephone conversation with James Sullivan on the morning of January 13, 1987, just three days before Lita was murdered.

After the questioning, I returned to the waiting room. Mike asked me how it went, and I told him it had gone okay. Mike and I then left the Russell Federal Building.

As I drove back to the hotel, I began trying to put more pieces of the puzzle together. My investigative mind was activated. I began to examine each question that was put to me during the interview with the authorities. It was obvious that they believed that Jim's telephone call to me had something to do with Lita's murder. Did the authorities assume that there was some kind of conspiracy between Jim and me? I tried to work the case as if I were the lead investigator.

Because I did not have access to some critical information, I had to substitute speculative scenarios for factual or presumed factual information. I had saved news articles regarding Lita's murder and the investigation. Comparing the questions with the information from the news articles, it was obvious that there were missing links. Apparently, the authorities were having the same problem. One thing was for certain—the authorities could no longer arrest me for Lita's murder, even if they suspected that I had something to do with it, which I did not.

Later that evening, I began to think about all the support and comfort that Mike Mears had given me for nearly five years. I know that Mike does not have divine powers, but I felt comfort in talking to him about the investigation. He made me feel that everything would one day be okay. Maybe there was some type of spiritual or divine intervention that resulted in Mike Mears representing me as legal counsel in the wiretap case, which led to him representing me now. However it happened, I was appreciative of Mike's comfort and support.

The next day, I went to the FBI office to take the polygraph examination. The FBI examiner, Clifford Cormany, treated me as if I were a common criminal. I did not feel any respect from the moment I walked into his office. He talked down to me as if he assumed that I was guilty. I reviewed and signed two forms: a consent to interview and an interrogation advice-of-rights form.

After I was hooked up to the polygraph machine, Special Agent Cormany asked me a series of control test questions. Some of the questions were "known truth" questions, such as my name, date of birth, etc. Then there were a couple of the questions to test for true or false responses. I objected to one of the questions, which was, "Did you ever falsify a legal document while you were a state trooper"? I objected to this question because, while serving as a trooper with the New York State Police, I would sometimes reduce a driver's traffic violation from 80 mph to 70 mph. In some cases troopers have the authority to give warnings or reduce the violation. Cormany did not substitute the question, but said that he would note my objection.

There is one question in particular that I remember during the polygraph examination. "Are you protecting the identity of anyone involved in Lita Sullivan's death?" I answered, "No."

After the examination, Cormany went out to confer with another agent. A few minutes later, he walked back into the room and said, "The results of your polygraph examination indicates deception."

"I answered all of the questions truthfully," I responded in an angry elevated voice. I then asked, "Are you finished with the examination? If so, I'm leaving."

"You may leave if you like," he responded, so I left the FBI building.

On my way back to the hotel, I wondered if he were bluffing, or if the polygraph examination results were inconclusive. As I said, I did answer all of the questions truthfully. If the polygraph examination did in fact indicate deception, it had to be because of my thoughts and feelings towards the person I felt was responsible for Lita's death. In my mind, I was convinced that Jim Sullivan was responsible, especially because of the panicked telephone call that he made to me on the morning of January 13th.

Polygraph examinations or tests are designed to measure your heart rate, respiration, and other responses caused by the nervous system. The polygraph measures these changes just as you anticipate answering a question. Supposedly, if you decide to answer a question deceptively or untruthfully, your heart rate and respiration changes dramatically. And, also supposedly, if you are going to answer truthfully, there will be minimal changes, if any. If you honestly believe something to be true but do not have physical or factual evidence to support your belief, deception could be indicated if you answer "no." I felt that Jim Sullivan was involved with or caused the death of Lita Sullivan, but I could not answer yes because I did not have any physical or factual evidence.

The results of polygraph examinations only became admissible in a limited number of U. S. court jurisdictions in 2007, and the admissibility remains highly controversial. There are many variables that can affect the test and render it inconclusive, or yield false positive (deceptive) results. The irony is that Jim Sullivan supposedly took a private polygraph examination and passed. But he refused to take a polygraph examination administered by law enforcement officials.

I called Mike Mears and told him what happened during the polygraph examination. Mike said that he would be able to tell if the examination indicated deception after he received and reviewed the results of the test. Unfortunately, the FBI refused to provide us with a copy of the polygraph examination, ignoring numerous requests.

* * *

I stopped by the after-school daycare and picked up Ingrid and drove her home. I kissed her goodbye and I told her that I loved her and that I would see her again real soon. Her eyes began to fill with tears as she hugged me and said, "I love you daddy." I said, "I love you, too, sweetheart." Ingrid and I both disliked saying goodbye.

I drove to the airport and boarded my return flight to New York. I felt a sense of relief as I stepped off the plane. When I left New York for Atlanta, I had been a prime suspect in a murder case. And now, I would never be falsely indicted, convicted, or sentenced and executed for something that I had absolutely nothing to do with.

After returning home, I brought my family up to date regarding the investigation. Heather was glad that I had returned home. One day, while Heather and I were at my parents' house in Mount Vernon, the doorbell rang. My mother answered the door and I heard her say, "Hello, Renee." Renee walked into the living room and my mouth dropped. It was obvious to see that Renee was pregnant! There was so much tension in the room, you could have cut it with a knife. I stood up and said, "Heather, I would like you to meet a good friend of mine, Renee Guy. Renee, I would like you to meet my friend, Heather Jones." They were both cordial to each other, and the room went silent for a few moments.

My mother said, "I see that you are expecting. When is the baby due?"

"In four months," Renee responded.

"Who is the lucky father?" I asked. Renee then told me the father's name—and the tension in the room eased as we resumed our conversation. I had previously mentioned Renee's name to Heather, and I wondered if she initially thought the baby was mine. I could sense that Renee may have been disappointed to see me with someone else. I felt a little disappointed to see that Renee was pregnant. But I felt that it was my fault that we were not still together. I was so preoccupied with the investigation, I could not think of anything else. And now it seemed it was too late.

* * *

A few weeks later, I received a call from a good friend in Atlanta, Shirley Simmons, who said, "Marvin, James Booker is missing."

"What do you mean that he's missing?" I asked.

She said, "James Booker is missing and no one knows where he is."

I still could not process what Shirley was saying. "Did he leave town? Did something happen to him?"

"Nobody knows. One day he didn't show up for work. His secretary doesn't know anything," she added.

"I hope he's okay," I said.

Several years before he disappeared, Booker's behavior had dramatically changed. When he left the law firm of Kutak Rock & Huie, he was a well-respected litigation attorney in the Atlanta community. He had established his own practice and told me that he had purchased a building on Peachtree Street. Booker was always image conscious; but later, he seemed to become obsessed with his image in a negative way. He bragged about his Mercedes and his Rolls Royce. He was once cited for contempt of court because he missed a scheduled court hearing. He told the judge that he had to go to South Carolina to have his Rolls serviced. Booker also began representing known drug dealers and began frequenting a popular strip club in Atlanta. He once told me that he actually owned a percentage of the club.

A mutual associate of ours told me that he had stopped by Booker's office one day and Booker was bragging about having a plastic bag containing thousands of dollars in cash. He said Booker opened a desk drawer and pulled out a plastic bag full of money and placed it on top of his desk. The bag appeared to be damp, as if it had once been buried in the ground. He said Booker opened the bag and it was indeed filled with cash money of all denominations.

Numerous rumors began to circulate regarding Booker's disappearance. Some said that he had either been killed by drug dealers or the mob. Others said that Booker was on the run from the authorities or the mob or drug dealers, or all of the above. And finally, some said that he was in a federal witness protection program.

I could not help but wonder if Booker's disappearance had something to do with the IRS investigation I'd been told about. I also wondered if his attempt to obtain information from me about Lita's murder had something to do with the IRS and his disappearance. I had been certain that Booker was wearing a wire during our dinner meeting—and this brings up a very interesting point. It seems to be okay for the authorities to obtain information by using a wiretap or eavesdropping device, but it is illegal for a private citizen to use one on his home telephone, one that is in his own name. Placing a wiretap on one's home telephone is legal in some states and illegal in others. Just like the death penalty. In any event, I hoped that Booker was okay.

Then I received a call telling me that Jim Sullivan had been arrested after he lied to the police following a traffic accident. After striking another vehicle, Jim apparently convinced his wife Suki to tell the authorities that she had been driving. Although Suki told the police just that, they did not buy her story.

Jim apparently convinced Suki to say that she was driving because his license had been suspended (or revoked) due to his numerous moving violations. Jim drove fast and recklessly, almost as if he had a death wish. Jim was convicted of a felony for giving false information to the police and placed on modified house arrest and probation.

Later that year, Suki and Jim separated and their divorce proceedings began, but that was only the beginning of Jim's troubles. During the divorce proceedings, Suki testified that Jim admitted to having Lita killed! Needless to say, the authorities were very interested in hearing what Suki had to say, though some naturally believed that her statement was just a ploy for sympathy—a way to get more money for her divorce settlement.

Lita's parents, Emory and JoAnn McClinton, filed a $4 million wrongful death suit against Jim in a Florida court. The McClintons won the suit, but it was later overturned by a court of appeals. The verdict would later be reversed by a higher court, but collecting the settlement would prove to be a problem.

∞

CHAPTER 9: JAMES VINCENT SULLIVAN'S FEDERAL INDICTMENT FOR THE MURDER OF LITA SULLIVAN

The following affidavit was submitted to a Florida magistrate in order to obtain a search warrant for Jim Sullivan's Palm Beach mansion. The affidavit was authored by FBI Special Agent Todd P. Letcher, who was one of the main FBI agents assigned to the murder case. This affidavit will provide details of the federal case that the FBI was building against Jim Sullivan.

Some of the details listed in the affidavit are false; there are some typographical errors; I am also skeptical and doubtful of some of the other details contained in the affidavit, but I will present the affidavit as submitted to the Florida magistrate. Even the address of the town-house where Lita was murdered is incorrect. The correct address is 3085 Slaton Drive, not 980. I will comment more on the affidavit after other documents are presented.

AFFIDAVIT

I, Todd P. Letcher, being duly sworn, depose and state the following:

INTRODUCTION

1. I am a Special Agent (SA) with the Federal Bureau of Investigation (FBI) and have been so employed for over five years.

2. I make this affidavit in support of an application for a search warrant to search the premises located at 920 SOUTH OCEAN BOULEVARD (AT THE INTERSECTION OF VIA BELLERIA) in PALM BEACH FLORIDA. The premises is described as a Mediterranean style mansion constructed of coral stone. The affidavit is based upon my personal knowledge and upon information provided to me by individuals I have interviewed in regard to the investigation described below.

THE OFFENSE UNDER INVESTIGATION

3. Lita McClinton Sullivan, a black female, was killed on January 16th, 1987. The cause of death was attributed to a gun shot wound to the head. Ms. Sullivan was shot in the foyer of a townhouse located at 980 Slaton Drive in Atlanta, Georgia, which was jointly owned by her and her estranged husband James V. Sullivan. James V. Sullivan, who is white, lived at that time and continues to live in the residence which is the subject of this search warrant application.

4. Eye witnesses to the murder told investigators that they observed an individual posing as a flower delivery man knock on Ms. Sullivan's door shortly before 8:15 a.m. on January 16, 1987. The witness stated further that when Ms. Sullivan answered the door, the flower delivery man was admitted inside the town home. The witness stated shortly thereafter they heard gunshots. They then saw the man run away from the Sullivan town house and out the entrance of the town home complex. The eye witness at the town home complex saw only one person at Lita Sullivan's door.

5. Investigators working the homicide found a box of flowers in the foyer where Ms. Sullivan was shot. The investigators traced the box to a Botany Bay Flower Shop. Randall Benson, an employee at the flower shop, told the investigators that he had sold that particular box of flowers to two individuals at approximately 7:45 a.m. to 8:00 a.m. on the morning of 1/16/87. Benson stated that one individual entered the store to purchase the flowers, while the other waited outside in a white Toyota. The open, passenger-side door gave Benson a good side view of the Toyota's driver. Benson told the investigators that he was certain it was the same box of flowers. He noted that only 5 of the 12 roses in the box that he was shown had been wired. He remembered that he had only wired 5 of the 12 roses for the men in the Toyota, because the individual who came in the store was starring at him so intently, he was too nervous to finish wiring the entire dozen roses. Benson provided police with detailed descriptions of both individuals. A police artist sketched drawings of the two individuals based upon the descriptions given by Benson.

6. The description of the two men who purchased the flowers and did not match that of the gunman who delivered them, thus investigators and affiant had concluded that three men were involve in the murder of Ms. Sullivan.

7. Neighbors living in the town home community where Ms. Sullivan was killed told investigators that during the early morning hours of January 13, 1987, they heard loud
knocking at Ms. Sullivan's door that lasted 10 to 15 minutes. To their knowledge Ms. Sullivan had not answered the door on that occasion. No description of the individual or individuals who were at Ms. Sullivan's door on the 13th was obtained.

THE INVESTIGATION REGARDING JAMES V. SULLIVAN

8. Lita Sullivan's husband, James V. Sullivan, has been a suspect in his wife's murder from the beginning of the investigation. At the time of the murder, the Sullivans were legally separated and were going through divorce proceeding. One of the issues in the proceeding was

a post-nuptial agreement which limited Lita Sullivan's share of the property division from the marriage. The validity of the post-nuptial agreement was hotly contested between the parties. A hearing on the agreement was scheduled for the afternoon of the day that Lita Sullivan was killed. A second matter pending at the time of the murder involved the status of a million dollar mortgage on Sullivan's residence in Palm Beach, Florida. This is the same residence that is the subject of this search warrant application. In approximately February of 1987 Sullivan was due to pay off a balloon mortgage on the house of approximately one million dollars ($1,000,000.00). Prior to January, 1987, he had applied for a new mortgage on the house in order to raise the funds needed to pay off the balloon note. The lending institution would not approve him for a mortgage without his wife's signature, because she was listed on the deed as a co-owner of the house. Lita Sullivan had refused to sign the refinancing papers and the divorce was not going to be final until after the note was due. Thus, Sullivan risked losing the house, which was appraised at as much as three million dollars ($3,000,000.00), because of his wife's refusal to participate in the refinancing of the residence. Finally, in a divorce settlement or trial Lita Sullivan stood to gain ownership of the town house where she was killed, which was appraised for approximately six hundred thousand dollars ($600,000.00), as well as the furnishing and artwork in the town house which were worth about two hundred thousand dollars ($200,000.00).

9. A friend of James Sullivan's Ed Wheeler, told investigators that Sullivan told him that there would be scorched earth tactics employed in the divorce. Wheeler understood Sullivan to mean that he did not want his wife to receive any of the property as the result of the divorce.

10. Sullivan had a long affair with Tanya Tanksley of Macon, Georgia, during his marriage to Lita Sullivan. Infidelity was one of the grounds raised by Lita Sullivan in her divorce petition. Vickie Durden, JoAnne Amos, and Judy Thompson, all acquaintances of Tanya Tanksley's, have told investigators that shortly after Lita Sullivan's murder, Ms. Tanksley told each of them the following: she was contacted by Lita Sullivan shortly before her death and was asked about

her affair with James Sullivan. Ms. Sullivan told her that she would be subpoenaed as a witness in the upcoming Sullivan divorce trial. Ms. Tanksley said that she then called James Sullivan and told him about her conversation with his wife. Sullivan told her not to worry about testifying, that he was going to take care of things. After Lita Sullivan was murdered, James Sullivan told Ms. Tanksley, "See I told you I'd take care of things where you wouldn't have to testify." Ms. Tanksley now denies that the above statements were made by her or to her three friends.

11. Telephone toll records reveal the following:

a. a telephone call from James Sullivan's residence in Palm Beach, Florida, to the residence of Marvin Marable in Atlanta, Georgia, on January 13, 1987, made at 7:02 a.m.;

b. a telephone call lasting between two and three minutes made from room 518 at the Howard Johnson motel located at 5793 Roswell Rd. in Atlanta, Georgia, to James Sullivan's residence in Palm Beach, Florida, at 7:44 a.m. on January 13, 1987;

c. two telephone calls from James Sullivan's residence to the office of Robert Christiansen in Atlanta, Georgia, made on January 13, 1987, at 8:58 and 9:31 a.m.;

d. a telephone call from Sullivan's residence in Palm Beach to the Howard Johnson on Roswell Rd. in Atlanta, on January 13 1987, at 10:33 a.m.;

e. a collect telephone call lasting approximately one minute made from a pay telephone at the Suwanee Rest Stop on Interstate 85 north of Atlanta to James Sullivan's residence in Palm Beach, Florida, at 9:00 a.m. on January 16, 1987.

12. Robert Christiansen is a lawyer who practices with a firm in Atlanta. In January 1987, he lived in the same town home complex as did Lita Sullivan. He was acquainted with James Sullivan, but had not talked with him in more than a year. On January 13, 1987, Sullivan called him at the office, and inquired about whether he had seen anyone knocking on Lita Sullivan's door at around four or five that morning. Christiansen had not seen anyone and told Sullivan that he had not. Later Christiansen did discover that other neighbors

*had heard loud knocking at the Sullivan residence that morning,
however, Christiansen did not tell Sullivan this.*

*13. After Lita Sullivan's murder, James Sullivan told Robert Chris-
tiansen that he had heard from the Atlanta Police Department that
his wife had been killed with a .9millimeter automatic weapon with
a seven round clip. In fact ballistics tests established that the murder weapon was a .9 millimeter automatic, however no one from
the Atlanta Police Department recalls telling Sullivan about the murder weapon. Atlanta Police reports do not mention this information
being provided to Sullivan.*

*14. The Suwanee Rest Stop on Interstate 85 is approximately
38 miles from the Sullivan town house in Atlanta where Lita Sullivan
was killed. The telephone call made to James Sullivan's residence
from there was approximately 45 minutes after Lita Sullivan was
shot. The approximate driving time from the Sullivan town house in
Atlanta to the rest stop is 45 minutes.*

*15. The room registration receipt from room 518 at the Howard
Johnson motel located at 5793 Roswell Rd. in Atlanta for January 13,
1987, provides the following information: the registrant for the room
used the names Johnny Furr, a party of three registered for the
room, the party of three checked in for the room at 7:24 a.m. on
January 13, 1987, the address listed is RT 40-1, Raleigh, North
Carolina 28112, the party paid cash for the room for one day, the
party did not check out at the desk when they left, and the party
listed their vehicle as a 1985 Toyota with North Carolina tags however, no tag number was listed. A long distance telephone call to
James Sullivan's residence in Florida was made from room 518
at 7:44 a.m. on January 13, 1987, however, the call was billed to
another, unknown number.*

*16. The configuration of the hotel is such that the cars of register-
ing guests are visible from the registration desk, therefore, it seems
likely that the guest registering as Johnny Furr correctly listed the car
on the receipt as a Toyota. As noted above Randall Benson identified
the car being driven by the purchasers of the flowers found near Lita
Sullivan's body as a white Toyota.*

17. The address listed on the registration receipt for room 518 appears to be false. The zip code listed is not in use by the United States Postal Service. The information provided is too sketchy to use to locate the registrant.

THE INVESTIGATION REGARDING THOMAS BRUCE HENLEY

18. A confidential informant (CI) has advised the investigators that Thomas Bruce Henley told him (CI) that he (Henley) and another individual, whose identity was unknown to the CI, but who was with Henley at the time, were involved in the murder of a black woman living in Atlanta who was married to a white millionaire living in Florida. The CI stated further that Henley told him that he had a lot of money because he and others had been paid by the black woman's husband to commit the murder. The informant also stated that the individual with Henley was a black male. The informant was not aware of the identity of the victim, but based upon the information provided by the informant, other investigators and I have concluded that the murder could only have been the Sullivan murder.

19. A photographic line-up of 11 individuals was shown to Randall Benson. Included in the photo array was a photograph of Thomas Bruce Henley. Benson picked out Henley's photo as looking "just like the driver" of the white Toyota.

20. The informant was shown a photographic line-up which included the picture of Marvin Marable. The informant picked Marable's photograph out of the photo line-up as being the black male who was associated with Henley in the Sullivan murder.

21. Marvin Marable is known to the investigators to be an associate of James Sullivan's. Marable pleaded guilty in the Superior Court of Fulton County to illegally wire-tapping Marable's wife's telephone. Incidental to this wiretapping scheme, Marable taped conversations involving Lita Sullivan. James Sullivan admitted that he received from Marable illegal tape recordings of conversations involving his wife.

22. Because of Marable's ties to James Sullivan regarding the wiretapping scheme, Marable was already considered a possible suspect in

the Sullivan murder. However there had not been any prior publicity of the information linking Marable to the Sullivan murder investigation. 23. The informant provided additional details about Marvin Marable that had been corroborated by the investigators. The informant stated that he had been taken to Marable's house in the Sandy Springs area of Atlanta. He gave the investigators directions to the general area where the house Marable was living was located. The investigators independently corroborated the fact that Marable did live in the area that the informant identified. However, the informant has failed an FBI administered polygraph examination. In the polygrapher's opinion the informant showed deception in responding affirmatively to the questions, "Did Henley tell you he and Botts did a contract hit on a woman in Atlanta?" and "Did Henley say his black associate set the hit up at the request of a wealthy man in Florida?"

THE EVIDENCE SOUGHT PURSUANT TO THIS SEARCH WARRANT APPLICATION

24. On August 16th, 1991, John Connolly, contributing Editor with Spy Magazine, and a former New York City police detective, advised affiant that James Sullivan recently invited Connolly to spend a week with him at his home in Palm Beach, Florida, as a guest. Connolly did so from July 27th, 1991 until August 3rd, 1991.
25. Connolly advised affiant that based upon the week he spent with Sullivan, Connolly came to believe that Sullivan is a very compulsive person, especially with regards to record keeping. Sullivan told Connolly he keeps a daily diary of his activities. The diary includes his plans for each day, the people he sees and talks to, and meetings that he attends. Sullivan also told Connolly that he has kept his diaries going back "forever". Sullivan told Connolly that from his diaries he was able to reconstruct the number of times that he had met with George Bissell, a former business associate. Sullivan stated that the number was exactly 109 times dating back to 1985.
26. Sullivan emphatically told Connolly that he maintains all of his records and does not destroy them. Sullivan also stated that he spent

at least two hours per day with his documents "getting his things in order". Sullivan also stated, "I keep everything in order until I finish with it and then I file it." Sullivan maintained that he still had every dress suit that he had bought since he was in high school.

27. On August 1, 1991 Sullivan gave Connolly a tour of Sullivan's "wing" of the house. Sullivan's wing included a master bedroom suite containing the master bedroom and bathroom, an office, a dressing room and a spare bedroom. Connolly observed that in the spare bedroom there was a bed that was piled high with various stacks of documents. Also in the room were several tables which had stacks of documents piled on them. The documents appeared to be stacked neatly. Connolly estimated the documents would fill at least 10 legal sized boxes.

28. Connolly also observed Sullivan's office which contained a desk which had several, neatly stacked, piles of documents on it. The office contained at least one filling cabinet. Connolly stated that Sullivan maintained a personal telephone directory along with other papers containing various telephone numbers. Included in the piles of documents which Connolly observed were legal papers, bills, and correspondence.

29. Connolly stated that he saw at Sullivan's house the diary on which Sullivan was currently working. Connolly believes that he may have seen Sullivan's previous diaries being kept in a filing cabinet in the office in the master suite in his home.

30. During the week that Connolly stayed at Sullivan's house, Sullivan was serving a sentence of home confinement arising from his conviction in Palm Beach County for subordination of perjury. Connolly observed that Sullivan did not go out to any other office nor did Sullivan mention having another office away from his home. Based upon affiant's investigation, Sullivan is not known to have an office away from his home, nor is he known to have any kind of storage facility for office records away from his home.

31. Sullivan related to Connolly that Marvin Marable had sent him over 300 hours of tape recorded conversations which related to Sullivan's deceased wife, Lita Sullivan's, extra marital affairs and other personal information. Sullivan first stated that he still had the tapes, but later he told Connolly that he sent them to his divorce lawyer.

As I mentioned earlier, I do not know Johnny Austin Turner, Clinton Botts, Thomas Bruce Henley, or Johnny Furr. How the FBI linked me to these individuals is a mystery. How did someone that I did not know, supposedly pick me out of a photo line-up? How did he supposedly tell the authorities the general location of my house in Sandy Springs and convince them that he had been there? None of the other witnesses identified seeing an African-American (black male) with the other subjects suspected of being involved with Lita's murder, not the hotel clerk, not the florist, not Robert Christenson, and not any other of the eye witnesses. So why did the FBI believe career criminal con-man Johnnie Austin Turner, especially after they admitted that he failed the polygraph examination?

Keep in mind that the authorities provided the media with statements from this individual which all but destroyed my credibility and painted me as a co-conspirator in Lita's murder. How could this happen in America? Unfortunately, it happens every day. Some authorities are so anxious to arrest and convict someone that they have targeted to be a suspect, they are willing to overlook crucial information and substitute it with speculation and lies.

Think about this: How would you feel if the authorities associated you with a murder that you had nothing to do with and the media reported that you were a suspect in the murder? How would you feel? Unfortunately, innocent people have been arrested, tried, convicted, and even executed based on circumstances such as these. Later in this book, you will see that some of the tactics used by the authorities bordered on being criminal.

The affidavit for a search warrant was sworn to in front of a magistrate and signed by FBI agent Letcher. Based on the affidavit, a search warrant was issued and executed at Jim's Palm Beach mansion. The authorities carted off boxes of documents and four weapons, which were in direct violation of Jim's probation as a convicted felon. In addition to serving some jail time, Jim was sentenced to eighteen months of modified house arrest and forty-two months of probation. While Jim was in jail, he was assaulted by another inmate and his nose was broken. It was also rumored that Jim had admitted to an inmate that he had had Lita killed.

The investigation had come to a dead end with numerous false leads, including those offered by Johnny Austin Turner. The FBI was desperate and wanted to indict Jim Sullivan before the expiration of the federal statute of limitations. That's why the U.S. Attorney's Office granted me forced immunity. Their strategy was to get enough information on Jim Sullivan to establish a credible case against him before the federal statute expired. But their strategy backfired when I informed them that I did not know any of the details regarding the death of Lita Sullivan. The other part of their plan fell apart when Turner falsely implicated Thomas Henley and Clinton Botts and then associated them with me.

The U.S. Attorney's Office was faced with a dilemma because they did not have enough evidence for a murder indictment in state court. The FBI had to either drop their five-year investigation or take their chances and have the U.S. Attorney's Office indict Sullivan under the use of interstate commerce to commit murder statute.

In January of 1992, just days before the expiration of the statute of limitations, the U.S. Attorney's Office issued a five-count indictment against James Vincent Sullivan, citing his use of interstate commerce to facilitate the murder of Lita Sullivan, meaning that some of the telephone calls Jim made and received were considered a form of interstate commerce. Much of the information in the affidavit to obtain the search warrant was used to obtain an indictment, after it was presented to the federal grand jury. At the time of the indictment Sullivan was still in a Florida jail for the violation of his probation. The five-count indictment lists the charges as follows.

IN THE UNITED STATES DISTRICT COURT
FOR THE NORTHERN DISTRICT OF GEORGIA
ATLANTA DIVISION

UNITED STATES OF AMERICA : CRIMINAL ACTION
v. : 1:92-CR-006
JAMES V. SULLIVAN :

THE GRAND JURY CHARGES THAT:

COUNT ONE

On or about January 13, 1987, at approximately 7:44 A.M., in the Northern District of Georgia, the defendant, James V. Sullivan, did knowingly and intentionally cause another to use interstate communication facility, to wit: a long distance telephone call between Atlanta, Georgia and Palm Beach, Florida, with the intent that the murder of Lita Sullivan be committed in violation of the laws of the State of Georgia as consideration for an agreement and promise to pay a thing of pecuniary value, and as consideration for the receipt of a thing of pecuniary value, said offense resulting in the death of Lita McClinton Sullivan, in violation of Title 18, United States Code, Section 1952A.

COUNT TWO

On or about January 13, 1987, at approximately 10:33 A.M., in the Northern District of Georgia, the defendant, James V. Sullivan, did knowingly and intentionally cause another to use interstate communication facility, to wit: a long distance telephone call between Palm Beach, Florida and Atlanta Georgia , with the intent that the murder of Lita Sullivan be committed in violation of the laws of the State of Georgia as consideration for an agreement and promise to pay a thing of pecuniary value, and as consideration for the receipt of a thing of pecuniary value, said offense resulting in the death of Lita McClinton Sullivan, in violation of Title 18, United States Code, Section 1952A.

COUNT THREE

On or about January 13, 1987, at approximately 10:38 A.M., in the Northern District of Georgia, the defendant, James V. Sullivan, did knowingly and intentionally cause another to use interstate communication facility, to wit: a long distance telephone call between Atlanta, Georgia and Palm Beach, Florida, with the intent that the murder of Lita Sullivan be committed in violation of the laws of the State of Georgia as consideration for an agreement and promise to pay a thing of pecuniary value, and as consideration for the receipt of a thing of pecuniary value, said offense resulting in the death of Lita McClinton Sullivan, in violation of Title 18, United States Code, Section 1952A.

COUNT FOUR

On or about January 16, 1987, in the Northern District of Georgia, the defendant, James V. Sullivan, did knowingly and intentionally cause another to use interstate communication facility, to wit: a long distance telephone call between Suwanee, Georgia and Palm Beach, Florida, with the intent that the murder of Lita Sullivan be committed in violation of the laws of the State of Georgia as consideration for an agreement and promise to pay a thing of pecuniary value, and as consideration for the receipt of a thing of pecuniary value, said offense resulting in the death of Lita McClinton Sullivan, in violation of Title 18, United States Code, Section 1952A.

COUNT FIVE

On or about January 16, 1987, in the Northern District of Georgia, the defendant, James V. Sullivan, in relation to a crime of violence for which he may be prosecuted in a court of the United States, to wit: the offenses charged in Counts One through Four of the instant indictment, did cause others to use and carry a firearm, in violation of Title 18, United States Code, Sections 924(c) and 2(b).

The indictment was signed by United States Attorney Joe D. Whitley, Assistant United States Attorney William L. McKinnon, Assistant United States Attorney Robert F. Schroeder, and the federal grand jury foreperson. The indictment indicated that it was a "TRUE BILL." The indictment also indicated that the document was filed in chambers on January 10, 1992, by the deputy clerk.

I received several calls from Atlanta advising me that Jim Sullivan had been indicted for arranging the death of Lita Sullivan. Mike Mears also called to say that the trial probably would not begin until the fall of the year. I put a few more pieces of the puzzle together. Now I knew why the authorities suspected that I was somehow involved with Lita's murder. It was the timing of the telephone call that Jim Sullivan made to me in the early morning of January 13, 1987. The authorities tried to connect the call that Jim made to me with the other calls that he received and made on January 13, 1987. They also (wrongly) connected me to the murder because of the false witness Johnny Austin Turner. Speaking of Turner, the authorities took him out of jail, because he (Turner) conned them into believing that he could lead them to the murder weapon. The following document is a synopsis of what transpired. The document was transcribed as written, including the mistakes.

AT 49-1027
JRK/mkw

I

On April 24, 1991, Special Agent JOHN R. KINGSTON and JAMES WAGON took substitute custody of JOHNNY AUSTIN TURNER, white male, date of birth May 28, 1952, from the United States Marshals and brought him to the Atlanta FBI Office.

Turner attempted to make contact with Bruce Hensley and Tim Botts telephonically. Eventually, he was told that a girl named TAMMY (Last Name Unknown) at the Smyrna Trailer Court would know where TIM BOTTS would be. He was taken to that location. SA KINGSTON met with the Atlanta Surveillance squad near that location.

A male at the trailer park in Unit B-2 told TURNER that both TIM and CLINTON BOTTS were down at Hillcrest Trailer Park further down Atlanta Road about one mile south of the intersection of Atlanta Road and Lattimer.

TURNER went there, and claimed he found TIM and CLINTON BOTTS in the last trailer on the left down the road (in the trailer park) just south of the three phone booths heading west and perpendicular to Atlanta Road.

TIM BOTTS allegedly told TURNER he would have someone bring the gun in a couple of hours. This conversation took place at 5:20 p.m. TURNER told BOTTS he would go home and come back later and then left and rejoined SA KINGSTON in his car.

TURNER returned to the trailer and the gun had not yet been delivered, so he told BOTTS he was going to get some cigarettes and call someone at the store across the street. TURNER instead came back to SA KINGSTON's car. After waiting approximately one-half hour, TURNER went back and failed to return to SA KINGSTON's vehicle at the time he was told. Each time TURNER made a trip into the trailer park he had been reminded that he was in custody, that he had a specific time he had to return within (5-10 minutes, 5-10 minutes, and 15-20 minutes respectively), and that should he attempt to escape, the consequences would be severe.

Nevertheless, TURNER failed to return after the third trip.

EXHIBIT "L"

* * *

Turner was also wearing a wire when he escaped. Several days later, the wire was recovered in the bathroom of a motel lounge. Turner was later apprehended and convicted of escape and destruction of government property. Turner had at least thirty-eight prior convictions, mostly felonies. Can you believe that this is the individual that convinced the FBI that he knew me and that he had been to my house? Did the authorities actually believe Turner when he told them that I was in some way connected to Botts and Henley? Were the authorities that desperate? Even after they discovered that Turner did not have any credibility, they did not issue a retraction statement to the media. Also, Thomas Bruce Henley was arrested in connection with the murder of Lita Sullivan but was later released due to lack of evidence to proceed with a trial. Clinton Botts was not arrested in connection with Lita Sullivan's murder.

James Vincent Sullivan, Lita McClinton Sullivan, Poppy Finley Marable and Marvin D. Marable, at the Marable's engagement party at Callanwolde Fine Arts Center in Atlanta

Callanwolde Fine Arts Center in Atlanta

The Marables' Residence in Sandy Springs at Powers Lake

The Sullivans' Palm Beach mansion

Marvin D. Marable

The Marable's wedding reception; Poppy Marable, Marvin Marable and
Lita Sullivan greeting guest

The Marables at their Powers Lake Residence

Marvin D. Marable, New York State Trooper

Marvin D. Marable, CEO of Bel-Mar Corporation

The Sullivans' townhouse in Buckhead

Marvin D. Marable and his wife Heather

Phillip Anthony Harwood during murder trial; Harwood was convicted
earlier of murdering Lita McClinton Sullivan

James Vincent Sullivan in court during the murder trial of Lita
McClinton Sullivan

∞

CHAPTER 10:
THE FEDERAL MURDER TRIAL

In October 1992, I received a subpoena to appear in Atlanta's Federal District Court to testify as a witness for the prosecution in the trial of James Vincent Sullivan. The trial began during the first week of November; I was scheduled to testify on November 4th.

I arrived at the courthouse at 2:30 p.m. and was directed to the witness waiting room. After waiting for about two hours, I was advised that I would not be called that day and was asked to return to court the following day.

On November 5th, I arrived at the federal courthouse building at 9:15 a.m. and met with Assistant U.S. Attorneys McKinnon and Schroeder and FBI Agent Letcher. After a brief meeting, I was directed to the witness waiting room. On my way to the waiting room, I saw Lita's mother JoAnn McClinton. I looked at her and acknowledged her, knowing that she would not speak. But to my surprise, she spoke to me and was quite cordial. Perhaps she felt differently about me since she knew that I was a witness for the prosecution. But did she still think I was in some way involved in the death of her daughter? I was reasonably sure that the authorities had told Mrs. McClinton about the early morning telephone call that Jim made to me on January

13, 1987. If the authorities had informed her of the telephone call—
and without her knowing the content of the call—she may have
assumed that I was somehow involved with Lita's murder. Before I
was granted use immunity, the authorities and others assumed that
I actually talked with Jim Sullivan when he called me on January 13th;
they were not aware that the call went to my voicemail and that I
called him back later from a friend's house.

Further down the hall, I saw Lita's father, Emory McClinton, and
her brother Emory, Jr. getting off the elevator. We acknowledged each
other, but their response to me seemed less than cordial.

I entered the waiting room and spoke to the other witnesses who
were waiting their turn to testify. Randall Benson, who was formerly
employed by Botany Bay Florist, was present. He sold the pink roses
to one of the co-conspirators. Benson was now living in California. A
representative was there from Southern Bell Telephone Company; a
representative from the Howard Johnson's Motor Lodge was present;
and Jan and Clyde Marlow were present. They were Jim's former
neighbors when he and Lita lived on Nottingham Drive in Macon,
Georgia. Jan Marlow and Lita had been very good friends.

Edward Garland, one of Jim's attorneys, walked into the waiting
room and asked to speak with me. I walked with him out into the
hallway, but I told him that I did not wish to discuss anything pertaining to the case with him. He kept insisting, and I kept telling him no.
He walked away disappointed. I did not want to talk with Jim's attorneys, because I did not want it to seem in any way that I was trying to
help him.

As I was about to walk back into the waiting room, I saw Jim Sullivan walking out of a conference room with his other attorney, Donald
Samuel. Jim walked by me and we made eye contact, and he acknowledged me, but we did not speak. I walked back into the waiting room,
wondering what Jim's attorney could possibly want to talk with me
about. I would find out later, and it would be shocking.

Finally, I was called to testify. I took a deep breath before I walked
into the courtroom, which was packed with spectators and the media.
Assistant U.S. Attorney Schroeder asked me to come forward to get

sworn in. There was a lot of commotion as I walked towards the witness stand. After being sworn in, I sat down and mentally prepared myself for the questioning. Schroeder began direct examination by asking me to state my name. He then asked me about the use immunity agreement. After several questions, Schroeder presented Judge Marvin Shoob with a new use immunity agreement, which would extend the immunity to cover my testimony during the trial. The jury was out of the room while the immunity agreement was signed. Jim's attorney Edward Garland and attorney Schroeder approached the bench and had a sidebar (private) discussion regarding the immunity agreement. Garland wanted to ask me questions pertaining to the immunity agreement, but Judge Shoob denied the request. The jury was then instructed to return to the courtroom.

Schroeder then began asking me questions about my background. He questioned me about my employment with the New York State Police, when I had moved to Atlanta, and when I met Lita Sullivan and Poppy Finley Marable. He then asked me about the wiretap recording device that I had placed on my home telephone. He asked me questions about informing Jim's divorce attorney John Taylor about the recording device and about discussions that I had had with Jim Sullivan regarding the tapes. Finally, he questioned me about the tapes that I mailed to Jim and my visit with him at his Palm Beach mansion. I gave testimony regarding the missing wiretap tapes, the ones that Jim had failed to return to me.

The next round of questioning focused on the financial arrangement that Jim and I had regarding his offer to pay me $30,000 if he did not have to pay more than the amount listed in the postnuptial agreement, which was approximately $250,000 in cash and other assets. I advised the court that I had not accepted any money from Jim Sullivan. Schroeder then asked me questions about Jim's pessimism regarding a favorable outcome of his divorce proceedings in Atlanta as opposed to Palm Beach.

Defense attorney Garland objected on numerous occasions during my testimony, stating that my opinion was speculation. On many occasions, the judge overruled Garland and permitted my testimony to stand. Eventually, Schroeder got around to questioning me about the early morning telephone call of January 13. I told the jury that Jim had left a voicemail message on my telephone, saying that it was urgent that I call him as soon as possible. I emphasized how Jim sounded desperate on the voicemail message. I told the jury that I was at a friend's house when I retrieved the message and that when I returned Jim's call, he was just as desperate-sounding as he had been on the recording, wanting to know if Lita still lived at the same address, if she still had the same car, and if anyone was living with her. I told the court that I did not provide Jim Sullivan with any of the information he was seeking.

After Schroeder finished his direct examination, Garland began his cross-examination. His questions initially focused on my memory regarding certain events and their dates. It was as if he were trying to discredit my memory, which would discredit my testimony. Garland asked numerous questions regarding information that I provided to Jim Sullivan from the tapes. He appeared to be trying to downplay the importance of the information obtained from the wiretap tapes.

Garland then began focusing on information I provided to Jim regarding Lita's dating or seeing other men, and her drug use. Someone had told me that Lita used cocaine, and I had relayed this information to Jim Sullivan. As I mentioned earlier in the book, I did not record any information that specifically confirmed that Lita was having sex with other men, nor did I have any direct knowledge of Lita using any drugs. It appeared to me that Garland was attempting to get me to state that I had direct knowledge of both. I told the court that I recorded the names of three men that Lita mentioned on the tapes.

The prosecution kept objecting to the way Garland was posing his questions, and Judge Shoob seemed to become frustrated with the way things were proceeding. The judge then asked me the following questions:

"Did you relate any information to Mr. Sullivan in these conversations that would have him believe that his wife was having affairs with other men?"

I responded, "Yes, maybe. I don't know if it was other men, but maybe another man, maybe yes."

Judge Shoob asked, "And did you relate any information to Mr. Sullivan that would lead him to believe that she was dating other men?"

I responded, "Yes."

Judge Shoob: "And how many men were involved, as far as the information you gave him?"

My reply: "As far as I know, and I'm not saying she was dating all of them, these were people that she talked to, there were three, as I mentioned before."

I did not feel comfortable testifying about whether or not Lita was having sex with other men. It appeared to me that Garland was trying to paint a picture of Lita as a loose woman. The term "affair" or "love affair" is broad, and does not necessarily imply sex. An affair can be emotional or sexual or both. The irony is that Jim Sullivan's defense team was seeking information about Lita's life after she had been legally separated, while Jim had documented affairs and sexual relations with other women while he and Lita were married and living together.

After Garland completed his questioning, Schroeder returned. He asked me to acknowledge that Lita Sullivan was separated from Jim Sullivan during the time that I had the wiretap device on my home telephone. Then Garland asked me to acknowledge that Lita was still married to Jim during the wiretapping.

Finally, after being grilled for several hours, I left the witness stand. Because I was a witness, I could not listen to the testimony of the others. The Southern Bell witness testified regarding telephone calls made during the time of Lita's murder. The florist testified regarding the two subjects observed during the purchase of the pink roses. And Jan and Clyde Marlow testified regarding a telephone call that they recorded when Jim called their residence, in which he describes the murder weapon. The Howard Johnson's clerk and other witnesses also testified.

It is safe to say that Jim's defense team considered me an adverse or hostile witness. I was truthful in my testimony, but I did not want to say anything that would appear to condone Jim's behavior. I had distanced myself from Jim Sullivan months before Lita was murdered, and afterwards I wanted to distance myself even further.

Jim's defense team submitted a motion to suppress evidence that was submitted by the U.S. Attorney's Office, citing that the evidence was defective and misleading. In a strange twist, Jim's attorneys discredited the bogus FBI confidential informant Johnnie Austin Turner, which gave credibility to my innocence. The motion to suppress refuted all of the libel and slanderous statements about me that were furnished to the media by the authorities.

Instead of me explaining how Jim's attorneys helped to restore my credibility, I am going to present the "Supplemental Motion to Suppress" that was submitted to the court on September 3, 1992, approximately two months before the trial began. Remember, I stated earlier in the book that the behavior of the authorities bordered on the criminal. I do not agree with all of the information in the motion; however, some of it is indisputable. The motion to suppress is presented here as it appeared and as submitted to the court, with the exception of a few obvious grammatical errors, which have been corrected. The motion reads as follows:

IN THE UNITED STATES DISTRICT COURT
FOR THE NORTHERN DISTRICT OF GEORGIA
ATLANTA DIVISION

UNITED STATES OF AMERICA,   :
Plaintiff,   :
v.   :   *CRIMINAL ACTION*
JAMES V. SULLIVAN,   :   *NUMBER: 1:92-CR-006*
Defendant.   :

DEFENDANT JAMES V. SULLIVAN'S AMENDED
SUPPLEMENTAL MOTION TO SUPPRESS

Defendant James V. Sullivan filed a Supplemental Motion To Suppress on September 1, 1992. This amended motion is being filed to incorporate specific references to the exhibits which are also being filed in support of the Motion To Suppress. There are, in addition, certain corrections which have been made to the original Supplemental Motion.

INTRODUCTION

On January 16, 1987, Lita Sullivan was killed when she opened the door of her house at approximately 8:15 in the morning. Her assailant, posing as a flower shop delivery man, handed her a dozen roses and then shot her in the head.

On September 5, 1991, FBI agent Todd Letcher signed an affidavit in connection with a search warrant application which was presented to a Magistrate in the Southern District of Florida (Exhibit "A"). The warrant, which was issued by the Magistrate, directed the agents to search the home of James V. Sullivan, the defendant in this case, who was married to, but in the process of obtaining a divorce from, Lita Sullivan at the time of her death. The search warrant affidavit purported to set out probable cause establishing that James Sullivan hired at least three men to kill Lita Sullivan and that evidence of this offense could be found in Sullivan's home in Palm Beach, Florida.

This motion seeks to suppress the evidence derived from that search and is based on material omissions and intentional misstatements contained in the search warrant affidavit. Franks v. Delaware, 438 U.S. 154 (1978). It is the contention of the defendant that but for the misrepresentations and omissions, there would have been no probable cause to support the issuance of the search warrant.

THE AFFIDAVIT

The affidavit is comprised of 31 paragraphs. Analytically there are seven different components of the affidavit which can be summarized as follows:

1. There are several paragraphs which set forth the known facts relating to this crime, such as the facts that the decedent lived in the house of James Sullivan (para. 3)"1", that she was shot in the head, and the assailant was posing as a flower delivery man (para. 4, 5). An eyewitness saw the assailant fleeing from the house and the man who sold the roses which were delivered to Lita Sullivan confirmed that he sold the flowers that morning (para 4, 5).

("1"Reference to the search warrant are designated by the paragraph number, "para. ___.")

We do not contest any of these facts.

2. The affidavit attempts to establish Sullivan's motive to commit the crime: (a) a hearing was set for that day to inquire into the validity of a post-nuptial agreement which would have restricted Lita Sullivan's right to James Sullivan's assets. (b) A balloon mortgage on the Florida property was due, but to refinance the note, Lita Sullivan's signature was needed, yet she refused to sign. (c) The divorce might have led to Lita acquiring ownership of the couple's Atlanta home (para. 8).

Most of this information is false. Actually, the balloon note had matured several months prior to the murder. (Exhibit "B"). Sullivan, alone, owned the Florida property and was at no risk of losing it because of any act, or failure to act on the part of Lita Sullivan. Actually, according to documents in the affiant's possession at the time he signed the affidavit, it was evident that Lita Sullivan had already agreed to sign the new mortgage (Exhibit "C"). Furthermore, the affidavit is inaccurate in stating that Lita Sullivan co-owned the Atlanta property. James Sullivan owned it alone (Exhibit "D"). There was virtually no possibility that Lita Sullivan would acquire an interest in the Atlanta property in light of the post-nuptial agreement.

3. The affidavit recounts how three friends of James Sullivan's erstwhile girlfriend (Tonya Tanksley) stated that Tanksley told them that Sullivan had told her that he would assure that Tanksley would not have to testify at the divorce trial, and that after the shooting, the defendant commented to her that he told her that she would not have to testify (para. 10).

This is false. The affidavit fails to state that Tanksley had testified under oath at the grand jury that this conversation never took place (Exhibit "E") and one of the girlfriend's friends has also denied that the conversation ever took place or that she ever told any agent that such a conversation was related to her by Tanksley (Exhibit "F").

4. The affidavit sets forth records of several phone calls, including a call from a Howard Johnson motel in Atlanta to Sullivan's house three days prior to the murder and a collect phone call from a rest-stop in Suwanee, Georgia, to Sullivan's home in Florida approximately 45 minutes after the shooting. With respect to the Howard Johnsons phone call, this is pertinent, according to the affidavit, because the room registration card was filled out by a man who indicated that he was from North Carolina (the address on the card is non-existent) and he was driving a Toyota, which according to the affidavit, was the same type of car the flower salesman claimed to have seen being driven by the purchaser of the roses. Thus, the type of car being driven by the flower purchasers is a critical link to the Howard Johnsons patrons who allegedly called Sullivan (para 11, 14, 15) (Letcher depo. At 106-107). "2"

("2" On August 27, 1992, FBI Agent Todd Letcher was deposed in a related case. References to his testimony are designated: "Letcher depo. at ____.")

This information is at best misleading and in substantial part, simply untrue. Actually the flower salesman originally stated that the car being driven by the purchasers was either a Honda or Toyota. Later, he clarified this and stated that it was definitely a Honda. Still later, he claimed it was an American car (a Mercury Lynx) (Exhibit "G"). The affidavit simply falsifies this information and fails to relate to the Magistrate the various identifications made by the flower salesman which are inconsistent with the government's theory of the case. This was a conscious decision on Letcher's part (Letcher depo. p. 39-42).

With respect to the phone call made from the Suwanee rest-stop it is conceivable that one can drive to that location in forty-five minutes from Buckhead. However, it is far from clear that the shooting occurred precisely at 8:15. The flower salesman, for example, stated that he did not open the shop until 8:05, making it unlikely that the shooting could have occurred at 8:15.

5. The affidavit refers to two calls between Sullivan and his Atlanta next-door neighbor, Robert Christiansen. The first related to Sullivan asking Christiansen about his knowledge of anybody knocking at Lita Sullivan's door early one morning, three days prior to the homicide. The second call occurred after the shooting, when Sullivan noted that he had heard that the murder weapon was a .9mm automatic (para 12, 13). This latter fact is pertinent, according to the affidavit, because at the time of the call, the type of weapon was not known to anybody outside of law enforcement.

This is false. The police had told Sullivan's lawyer what kind of weapon was used and the attorney had revealed this to Sullivan prior to the phone call (Exhibit "H").

6. The affidavit then plunges into a description of the information provided by a confidential informant. This informant, who has now been identified as Johnny Austin Turner, claimed to have been told by one of the assailants that he had committed the crime (para 18, 19, 20, 21, 22, 23). According to the informant the three assailants were Thomas Bruce Henley, Clint Botts and an unknown third person, but presumably "Johnny Furr" the person who checked into the Howard Johnson hotel. The arrangements were supposedly made by a friend of Sullivan's named Marvin Marable (Exhibit "I"). On the basis of Turner's revelations, the FBI provided a photographic line-up to the flower salesman, who identified Henley as "looking just like" the man who was waiting in the car when the flowers were purchased (para 19) (Exhibit "J"). The affidavit states that Marable had not previously been associated with the investigation publicly (thus bolstering the informant's credibility); and that Marable was picked out of a photographic line-up by Turner (para 20, 22).

This aspect of the affidavit is completely false, misleading and was consciously designed to mislead the Magistrate. To begin with, the affidavit fails to reveal the following information about Johnny Austin Turner:

a. Turner was arrested more than 30 times during the past fifteen years. He has spent the majority of the last 20 years in prison.

b. The affidavit does acknowledge that Turner failed a polygraph on two relevant questions ("Did Henley admit being the killer, along with Clint Botts?" and "Did Henley say his black associate set the hit up at the request of a wealthy man in Florida?") What the affidavit fails to reveal is that the polygrapher and a GBI agent who questioned Turner were convinced that he was not telling the truth; that Turner subsequently refused to testify at the grand jury even under a grant of immunity because of his fear of perjury; and that his statements prior to being polygraphed were inconsistent with other statements he made to law enforcement agents about the case. According to the Atlanta police, "Turner stated that he did not wish to perjure himself, a reference to his pending testimony before a Federal Grand Jury. The context of this statement was an admission on Turner's part that he had not been truthful." The affiant did not share these observation with the Magistrate in Florida (Exhibit "K").

c. Turner agreed to help the agents recover the murder weapon. To accomplish this, he convinced the agents to allow him to wear a "wire" and meet with Botts at Botts' house. When the agents allowed Turner to do this, Turner escaped, stealing the equipment. On the basis of this escapade, Turner was prosecuted and convicted in the United States District Court before Judge Horace Ward, United States v. Turner, 91-CR-163-HTW (N.D. Ga. 1991) (Exhibit "L"). The same FBI agent who signed the affidavit in this case was the agent in Turner's prosecution. The same assistant United States Attorney who prepared the affidavit in this case also prosecuted Turner for making false statements and stealing the equipment. When Turner was captured, he claimed he had been kidnapped (Letcher depo. at 109 - 110), which was a lie. All this information was hidden from the magistrate in Florida. Turner's trial and conviction for lying in connection with this investigation occurred just one month prior to the date the affidavit was presented to the Magistrate. Yet, none of this information was revealed in the affidavit.

d. In addition to Turner's remarkable criminal background in general, he had also engaged in similar schemes with law enforcement. In 1986, he convinced a district attorney in Savannah that he had information that a "contract" had been placed on his life by a man awaiting trial in a murder case. When the FBI concluded that this was totally fabricated by Turner, Turner wrote to the defendant's attorney and told him that the district attorney had induced him to lie in order to frame the murder defendant. The FBI confirmed that Turner's allegations were wholly unsubstantiated. This episode was not revealed to the Florida Magistrate.

e. When called to the grand jury, Turner refused to testify to the information related in the affidavit, relying on his right against self-incrimination. This was not revealed to the Florida Magistrate.

f. Turner had previously been an informant for Cobb County; however, based on his prior lies to that jurisdiction's law enforcement agents, he was no longer allowed to work on any cases there (Letcher depo. at 122) (Exhibit "M"). This was not revealed to the Florida Magistrate.

g. Turner's statements regarding his involvement with Henley, Marable and Botts was not consistent from one interview to the next. At first he stated that he met Henley and Marable at a bar on Stewart Avenue. Later, however, he claimed that he traveled with Marable and Henley to Florida where he met Sullivan (Letcher depo. at 127) (Exhibit "N").

The affidavit's statement that the flower salesman identified Henley is exaggerated. The salesman did not state that Henley looked "just like" the driver, as stated by the affiant in the affidavit. Rather, he stated "that this individual looked like the person who did the driving." He later clarified this by saying, he could not be positive of either the driver or the flower purchaser, but the pictures "definitely resembled the purchaser and the driver." In short, Letcher now concedes that, "If you mean [did he give] any positive identifications, I would say no." (Letcher depo. at 47). That's not *what he wrote in the affidavit, however (Exhibit "O"). Then, despite the fact that the affidavit suggest that Clint Botts and Henley bought the flowers (Botts came in the store, Henley remained in the car) and that "Furr" was the shooter, the affidavit fails to reveal that the flower salesman did not identify Botts as the purchaser, but instead identified a man named Faircloth (Exhibit "P"). This identification directly contradicts the information provided in the affidavit. Omitting this identification from the affidavit is beyond the realm of recklessness and amounts to a blatant effort to deceive the magistrate.*

7. The affidavit concludes with information provided by John Connolly, a reporter for Spy Magazine. The purpose of this information is to establish some connection between the crime which occurred almost five years previously and the location which was the subject of the search warrant. Connolly related to the affiant that Sullivan kept meticulous records of his life, dating back many years. The affiant assumes, therefore, that evidence of the murder could be found in the house.

What the affiant did not reveal to the Florida Magistrate was that Connolly had previously been an informant for the FBI in New York, but had been fired because he could not be trusted. Connolly had also been an informant for the United States Attorney's Office in the Southern District of New York, but again, had been fired for unreliability. Connolly had also been investigated by the Securities and Exchange Commission and allegations of fraud had been filed by the SEC against Connolly in 1983 and 1984.

Apart from these various omissions and misrepresentation, the affidavit also fails to inform the magistrate of these facts which were known to the affiant:

1. Sullivan had taken a polygraph test and passed, showing that he had no participation in the murder (Letcher depo. at 67 - 68) (Exhibit "Q");

2. One of Lita Sullivan's neighbors was a suspect in the murder. He had threatened to kill Lita and had driven his car through her garage door. He had also acknowledged to the police that he had been romantically involved with Lita (Letcher depo. at 59, 62) (Exhibit "R").

3. Sullivan has repeatedly agreed to give statements to the police when asked (Letcher depo at 69 - 70) (Exhibit "S").

4. Lita Sullivan was known to have been involved in the drug trade prior to her death and may have had contacts with organized crime. Atlanta Police believed at one point that her death was related to these associations (Exhibit "T").

The defendant is prepared to go forward at an evidentiary hearing and establish that the affidavit contains each of the aforementioned misrepresentations and material omissions. It is the contention of the defendant that if the material omissions had not been made and the intentional misrepresentations were corrected, the affidavit would no longer present a probable cause basis for issuing a search warrant. For this reason, an evidentiary hearing is necessary to inquire into the factual basis of this _Frank v. Delaware_ challenge.

MEMORANDUM OF LAW

The fourth Amendment protects people from unreasonable searches by requiring the authorization of a neutral detached magistrate before a search can be executed. _Lo-Ji Sales, Inc. v. New York_, 442 U.S. 319 (1979). Providing inaccurate information to the magistrate eviscerates this protection. The magistrate's function becomes a nullity. _Franks v. Delaware_, 438 U.S. 154 (1978). If the affidavit contains misrepresentations or material omissions, they must be disregarded in evaluating the probable cause foundation of the search. _United States v. Simpson_, 813 F.2d 1462 (9th Cir, 1987); _United States v. Melvin_, 596 F. 2d 492 (1st Cir. 1979); _United States v. Dennis_, 625 F.2d 782 (8th Cir. 1980); _United States v. Redmond_, 652 F.Supp. 747 (E.D.Cal. 1985). Misrepresentations about the information provided by an informant may be sufficient to taint the entire search warrant. _United States v. Baxter_, 889 F.2d 731 (6th Cir. 1989; _United States v. Bennett_, 905 F.2d 931 (6th Cir. 1990).

Here, as set forth above, there were countless misstatements about the information provided by Johnny Austin Turner and an intentional effort to shield from the magistrate a wealth of information about Turner's background and prior performance as an informant, as well as prior lies and misconduct in connection with this investigation. In several respects, the affidavit misstated the facts about the assets of the defendant and decedent, thereby falsely creating a motive for Sullivan to commit the crime. The affidavit falsely suggests that Sullivan could only have known about the murder weapon if he had been a participant, when, in fact, the type of weapon used had been revealed to his attorney. Also, the affidavit exaggerates the identification made by the flower salesman.

Furthermore, the failure to include in the affidavit information which contradicted the information contained in the affidavit may taint the entire warrant. Hale v. Fish, 899 F.2d 390 (5th Cir. 1990). Here the affidavit stressed the fact that the flower salesman claimed that the purchasers drove a Toyota. The affidavit fails to reveal that the salesman later changed his mind and claimed it was a Honda and still later settled on a Mercury Lynx. The affidavit failed to reveal that the girlfriend, under oath at the grand jury, denied that Sullivan had ever made a statement about her not having to testify at the divorce proceeding. The affidavit failed to reveal that Turner had made several inconsistent statements about the information provided him by the supposed hit man.

The fact that FBI Agent Letcher was relying on information provided by other law enforcement agents, moreover, is not relevant. Obviously, one law enforcement officer may not recklessly provide misinformation to the affiant and thereby shield the affidavit from scrutiny. As Franks makes clear, it is the obligation of the affiant to ascertain and present to the issuing judge all facts concerning the informant's reliability (and other information) that may have been within the knowledge of agents acting under his supervision. Franks, supra, 438 U.S. at 163-64 n. 6; United States v. Tufaro, 593 F.Supp. 476, 485-86 (S.D.N.Y. 1983): United States v. Dorfman, 542 F.Supp. 345, 366 n. 18 (N.D.Ill. 1982) (Where hearsay is provided

to one government agent who knows the informant is lying, recklessly believes the informant, or deliberately or recklessly misreports
the information to a second government agent, who then innocently
includes the misrepresentation in an affidavit, the government cannot
insulate one officer's deliberate misstatement merely by relaying it
through an officer-affiant personally ignorant of its falsity.)

The affidavit in this case makes a mockery of the requirement
that a neutral and detached magistrate decide whether there is
probable cause to issue a search warrant. Purposefully and with
design, the affiant manipulated the facts, intentionally misstated
numerous facts, intentionally omitted other facts which were highly
relevant to the issue and presented to the Magistrate in Florida an
affidavit which substantially distorted the truth as it was then known
to the affiant. The underlying purpose of <u>Franks</u> is clear:

> If the government could intentionally or recklessly omit
> the material facts from warrant affidavits and applications,
> the same danger [as presenting false statements] would be
> created. If the government had unfettered power to pick and
> choose which facts to present to the magistrate regardless
> of how misleading the presentations were, the magistrate's
> review of the affidavit would be rendered meaningless. The
> magistrate would not be provided with a fair opportunity to
> review the government's evidence in making the probable
> cause determination. He would perform his crucial role at
> the whim, caprice or duplicity of the governmental agents
> involved in the case.

Although the motion to suppress was filed with the court in September, Judge Shoob decided to go forth with the trial. I returned to
New York to wait for a verdict.

Less than a week later, I received a call from Mike Mears, telling
me that Judge Shoob had thrown the case out of court and acquitted
Jim Sullivan before the case went to the jury.

How could this have happened? The answer is easy: sloppy police
work. The motion to suppress made numerous references to the affi-

davit that had been submitted to the Florida magistrate to obtain a search warrant for Sullivan's Palm Beach home. I mentioned earlier that some of the information contained in the affidavit was not true or was misleading. Some of the same information was used to obtain an indictment of Jim Sullivan. The authorities had mixed good information with bogus information furnished by Johnny Austin Turner. Tainted information puts all information in jeopardy, which in turn calls into question the integrity (and competence) of the officials conducting the investigation. The motion to suppress threw into doubt some if not all of the information contained in the affidavit, and perhaps also affected evidence and testimony provided during the trial.

Jim Sullivan had one of the best defense teams in Atlanta. They knew exactly what they were doing, and they paid attention to all details. The foundation for questioning the integrity of the evidence submitted by the authorities and the prosecution was laid before the trial began. The motion to suppress was the trump card being held by Sullivan's defense team. After the trial had ended, but before the case went to the jury, Sullivan's defense team made a motion to the court to acquit Jim Sullivan on all five counts of the indictment. Judge Shoob initially deferred the ruling on the defense's motion. However, Sullivan's defense team said that the court was not permitted to defer a ruling at that stage of the trial. The court acknowledged the motion and, after considering the substance of the motion, granted an acquittal on all five counts of the indictment. According to Federal Rule of Procedure 29, the court was bound to rule on the motion before the case was presented to a jury. Some of the evidence that the Judge evaluated before making his ruling was contained in the motion to suppress.

Many people were upset and disappointed at Judge Shoob's ruling, but he acted in accordance with federal law. If the authorities had presented an airtight case, the defense's motion would have been dismissed, and the case would have gone to the jury. Remember, I said earlier that the authorities were desperate because the expiration date of the federal statute of limitations was fast approaching.

It is important that the reader understands why Judge Shoob acquitted Jim Sullivan; therefore, I am providing here, in full, the order acquitting him.

UNITED STATES DISTRICT COURT
NORTHERN DISTRICT OF GEORGIA
ATLANTA DIVISION

UNITED STATES OF AMERICA,	:	
Plaintiff,	:	CRIMINAL ACTION
v.	:	1:92-CR-006-MHS
JAMES "{S}" SULLIVAN	:	
Defendant	:	

ORDER

This order memorializes the Court's oral ruling of November 23, 1992, granting defendant's motion for judgment of acquittal. After hearing the evidence presented by the Government and argument on the motion, the Court concluded that the Government failed to establish that a reasonable juror could find beyond a reasonable doubt that the telephone calls charged in the indictment facilitated or related to the murder of Lita Sullivan as required by 18 U.S.C. - 1958.

BACKGROUND

Lita Sullivan was murdered on the morning of January 16, 1987, when she was shot by a man delivering flowers to her house in the Buckhead section of Atlanta, Georgia. The "trigger man" and his accomplices have not been apprehended or identified. Defendant, the victim's estranged husband, was at his home in Palm Beach, Florida, at the time of murder. In months preceding the murder, Lita Sullivan and defendant had been engaged in bitterly contested divorce proceedings. A hearing on the couple's postnuptial agree-

ment was set for the afternoon of Lita Sullivan's murder, and the divorce trial was scheduled for about two weeks later.

Telephone records show that three days before the murder, on January 13, 1987, a telephone call was made from a room at a Howard Johnson's motel in Sandy Springs, Georgia, to defendant's Palm Beach residence, and about three hours later a call was made from that Palm Beach residence to the Howard Johnson's. The records also show that the defendant made several calls that morning to a man who was Lita Sullivan's neighbor in Buckhead. He also called a mutual friend in search of Lita Sullivan's whereabouts. Finally, the records show that a collect call was made from a pay telephone at a rest stop on I-85 to defendant's Palm Beach residence on the day of Lita Sullivan's murder about 40 minutes after she was shot. The rest stop is about 30 miles from Lita Sullivan's house.

The Government indicted defendant under the federal murder-for-hire statute and charged him with making or causing to be made four telephone calls with the intent to murder Lita Sullivan. The two calls involved the Howard Johnson's motel, the call from the next door-neighbor, and the call from the rest stop are the calls listed in the indictment. Defendant was also charged with one count of causing another to use a firearm in a crime of 18 U.S.C - 924(c).

JUDGMENT OF ACQUITTAL

Defendant moved for judgment of acquittal on all counts under Federal Rule of Criminal Procedure 29 at close of the Government's case. After hearing argument, the Court deferred ruling on the motion and the trial continued. Defendant, however, brought to the Court's attention that under Rule 29, the Court is not permitted to defer ruling on a motion for judgment of acquittal at this stage. (1)

----

(1) (When a defendant moves for judgment of acquittal at the close of all of the evidence, Rule 29 (does not) permit the court to reserve judgment on the motion pending the jury verdict).

Accordingly, the Court agreed to reconsider its ruling upon defendant's "renewed" motion.

On a motion for judgment of acquittal, the district court "shall order the entry of judgment of acquittal . . . if the evidence is insufficient to sustain a conviction of such offense or offenses." Fed. R. Crim. P. 29(a). In weighing the evidence, the court must view the evidence in light most favorable to the Government and make credibility determinations in favor of the Government. Then the court must decide whether "a reasonable trier of fact could have found that the evidence established guilt beyond a reasonable doubt." United States v. Vidal-Hungria, 794 F.2d 1503 (11th Cir. 1986). As defendant points out, while a defendant "may be guilty, . . . his conviction cannot rest upon mere conjecture and suspicion." United States v. Fitzharris, 633 F.2d 416 (5th Cir. 1980).

COUNTS ONE - FOUR

Defendant was charged with four counts of using the telephone with the intent to commit a murder in violation "{of}" the federal murder-for-hire statute, 18 U.S.C. - 1958. The statute provides in part:

> Whoever . . . uses or causes another . . . to use the mail or any facility in interstate or foreign commerce, with the intent that a murder be committed in violation of the law of any State of the United States as consideration for the receipt of, or as consideration for a promise or agreement to pay, anything of pecuniary value, shall be . . . subject to imprisonment . . . .

18 U.S.C. - 1958. In deciding the motion for judgment of acquittal, then, the Court was required to consider whether, based on the evidence presented by the Government, a reasonable juror could find beyond a reasonable doubt (1) that defendant had the intent that Lita Sullivan be killed, (2) for money and, (3) that the telephone calls charged in the indictment facilitated or were related to the murder.

The primary question at issue here was whether the Government made the necessary showing of a connection between the telephone calls and the murder. (2)

Under 18 U.S.C. 1958, the use of a telephone or other means of interstate means of interstate commerce is a jurisdictional prerequisite; it is the hook into the federal jurisdiction for what would otherwise be a state crime. United States v. Edelman, 873 F.2d 791 (5th Cir. 1989); United States v. Perrin, 580 F.2d 730 (5th Cir. 1978), aff'd on other grounds, 444 U.S. 37 (1979). The use of the telephone, however, must be shown to relate to the murder. In this case, the Government must show that the telephone was "in fact used in the commission of that offense and that [defendant] had knowledge of the substantive offense which he promoted." Edelman, 873 F,2d at 795.

---

(2) In considering a motion for judgment of acquittal, the Court must make all credibility determinations in favor of the Government. Accordingly, based on the testimony defendant's third wife, Hyo-Sook ("Suki"), the court is able to find that a reasonable juror could find beyond a reasonable doubt that Sullivan had the intent to murder Lita Sullivan.

The actual application of this standard – that the telephone was "used in the commission" of the murder – is unclear. Defendant argued that this standard requires the Government to show that the telephone calls "facilitated" the offense. Since there is little case law on 18 U.S.C. - 1958, defendant urged the Court to interpret - 1958 in light of other statutes that criminalize the use of communication facilities, the mail, and travel. See 18 U.S.C. - 1952; 18 U.S.C. - 1343; and 21 U.S.C. - 843(b). Each of these statutes includes language setting forth the required nexus between the interstate activity and the underlying crime. (3)

---

(3) The Travel Act, 18 U.S.C. - 1952, criminalizes the use of interstate facilities to "promote, manage, establish, carry on, or facili-

tate" the unlawful activity. 18 U.S.C. - 1952 (a) (3). Another sub-section of the act, 18 U.S.C. - 1952 (a) (2), criminalizes the use of interstate facilities "with the intent . . . to commit any crime of violence to further unlawful activity."

The wire fraud statute, 18 U.S.C. - 1342, criminalizes the use of a wire, radio or television communication for "the purpose of executing" a scheme to defraud.

Also, 21 U.S.C. - 843 (b) criminalizes the knowing or intentional use of a communication facility in "committing or in causing or facilitating the commission" of various drug offenses.

The murder-for-hire statute, however, does not include such specific language. Thus the language and case law on these statutes are not dispositive.

The Government, on the other hand, contended that the statute requires the Government to show only that the telephone "relate to" the murder. As authority, the Government cited several cases holding that 1958 does not require a showing that a defendant specifically intended to use the interstate communication facility. For example, in the _Edelman_, the defendant hired someone to kill his wife, and the person he hired then used the mail to hire a hit man. The contents of the letters were known, and the relationship between the planned murder and the use of the "{mails}" was clear. The Fifth Circuit held that a defendant charged under 1958 did not need to specifically intend that the mail be used in the commission of the offense. _Edelman_, 873 F.2d 1140 (5th Cir. 1992) (reaffirming holding that the Government does not need to show specific intent to use the interstate commerce facility). Neither these cases nor others cited by the Government, however, provide authority that the evidence in this case showed that the calls listed in the indictment "related to" the killing.

If the analysis in _Edelman_ is applied to this case, a reasonable juror could not have concluded beyond a reasonable doubt that these calls related to, much less facilitated, Lita Sullivan's murder. Assuming that the Government had shown that Sullivan intended to have the murder committed, the Government did not show that the telephone calls related to the murder -- that is, that they were "in fact used in the commission of the offense." Although a juror could reasonably conclude that the defendant was a party to each of the four calls, the Government failed to establish who was the other party to the telephone calls made to and from the Howard Johnson's and from the Suwanee rest stop. There is no evidence showing who checked into the Howard Johnson's on January 13, 1987. (4)

---

(4) According to the motel's registration form, a party of three checked into the room which the call to Sullivan's residence was made. The person registering put down a non-existent North Carolina address. The motel clerk testified that the person drove a white car of Japanese make. During the trial, she was not asked to identify any of the drawing of the suspects made from descriptions given by other witnesses.

The Government produced no evidence linking the party staying at the Howard Johnson's with Lita Sullivan's murder on January 16 nor did it show who made and received the calls and what was said during those calls. The Government also failed to produce any evidence about the calls made from the rest stop and produced no evidence showing that the call to Lita Sullivan's neighbor on January 13 was connected to the murder on January 16. (5)

---

(5) Lita Sullivan's neighbor testified that the morning of January 13 defendant James Sullivan telephoned him several times. When the neighbor returned the calls, James Sullivan asked if the neighbor had noticed anything unusual at Lita Sullivan's house and if he had Lita Sullivan's telephone number.

With no evidence of the content and no evidence of identifying the other parties to these calls, no reasonable juror could have found beyond a reasonable doubt that the calls "were used in the commission of" the murder.

In oral argument, the Government relied on a Fifth Circuit case under the wire fraud statute, 18 U.S.C. - 1343, and argued that the Government was not required to prove contents of the telephone calls or to show with direct proof who made the call. <u>United States v. Shively</u>, 927 F.2d 804 (5th Cir. 1991). In <u>Shively</u>, however, the evidence showed that the defendant conspired to commit arson, that although the defendant initially denied that anyone was staying at her home, a three-minute telephone call from her hotel room had been made to her house only eighteen minutes after she checked into the hotel, and that the person staying in her house the night the call was made was the person who started the fire. Although the content of the call were not known in <u>Shively</u>, the parties to the call were known – or could be identified by a reasonable juror – and the Government had presented evidence that one of the parties had admitted starting the fire. Thus, <u>Shively</u>, does not support the Government's contention that the Government in this case produced enough evidence connecting the telephone calls with the murder of Lita Sullivan.

The Government failed to show that the telephone calls facilitated the murder of Lita Sullivan. The Government also failed to provide sufficient evidence that these telephone calls even related to the murder. Thus, the Court granted defendant's motion for judgment of acquittal on these charges, finding that no reasonable juror could have found beyond a reasonable doubt that the calls related to the murder.

COUNT FIVE

Defendant was also charged with causing a gun to be used in violation of U.S.C. - 924(c). This statute allows the federal prosecution of a person who causes a gun to be used "in relation to any crime of violence . . . for which he may be prosecuted" in federal court. Because the count found that there was insufficient evidence on the four telephone counts, which provided the federal jurisdiction in this matter, the Court granted the motion of acquittal on Count Five.

CONCLUSION

Accordingly, having considered the evidence presented at trial, the Court GRANTS defendant's motion for judgment of acquittal and DIRECTS that a judgment of acquittal be entered in this matter.

IT IS SO ORDERED, this 17th day of December, 1992.

Marvin H. Shoob, Senior Judge
United States District Court
Northern District of Georgia

I don't even know where to begin. First of all, I am sure that Mr. and Mrs. McClinton were furious about the judge's decision. I was very upset and disappointed. It felt as if a wealthy person had taken advantage of a legal loophole. The law is simple, but at the same time, it is very complex. Jim Sullivan, a wealthy individual with resources to hire the best attorneys in the business who would leave no stone unturned, a federal judge who respects the letter of the law and case law decisions, and the authorities, up against a federal statute deadline and forced to present a case with an informant that had *no* credibility, is a recipe for disaster. The three legal documents—the affidavit, the motion to suppress, and the order of judgment acquittal—along with the defense's oral argument say it all; so I needn't comment any further.

It seemed as if Jim had dodged the bullet due to the authorities mishandling the investigation. If I had been in charge of the investigation, I would have immediately focused on identifying the owner or driver of the white Toyota from North Carolina. I would have assigned one agent to investigate the vehicle through North Carolina's DMV. I would then have obtained information on everyone that Jim Sullivan came in contact with in the year preceding Lita's murder. I would have focused on felons that had been released from North Carolina's prisons and jails in the year preceding Lita's death. I would have tried to figure out what ties Jim had with anyone from North Carolina. I would have investigated money transactions of Sullivan's, particularly up to one year prior to Lita's death; then try to link those transactions to any potential suspects. Also, I would have canvassed the Buckhead neighborhood to see if anyone had seen or heard anything suspicious during the week leading up to Lita's murder. But unfortunately, I was not in charge of the investigation; to the contrary, I was a suspect. It was also unfortunate that the authorities were back to square one and had to start all over again. The case would soon go cold.

Before the trial began, Jim sold the Palm Beach mansion for $3.2 million and moved to the Boynton Beach area in Florida. I wondered if he thought that he had gotten away with murder.

* * *

Back in New York, I entered a graduate program in criminal justice at my alma mater Iona College. I continued government contract consulting as well. Heather and I were still dating, and our relationship had become serious. I had thought about leaving New York, but I did not want to move back to Atlanta, so I started exploring other options.

During a trip to Virginia, I stopped to get some gas while traveling on I-95 near Quantico. While at the gas station, I noticed a sign advertising a new real estate development. I decided to go to the sales office to get some information on the development and look at some of the model homes. I liked the development and took some information with me to review later. I drove around the area to get a better feel for the surroundings. Many of the residents in the area were active military, employed by federal government agencies or federal government contractors. The FBI academy and U.S. Drug Enforcement Administration were located in nearby Quantico, along with the Marine Corps. Washington, DC, was approximately forty miles away, which would make it easy for me to conduct my consulting business.

After I returned to New York, I reviewed the real estate information and did more research on the area. I then decided to purchase a townhouse in the complex. I started looking into employment opportunities in Virginia, specifically for a position that would allow me to continue my consulting. I decided to put graduate school on hold for a while.

Several months later, Heather and I were married, and we moved into the new townhouse in Virginia. Heather secured employment in Washington, but I opted not to become a frustrated commuter spending up to two hours each way, every day, in traffic. You will never guess in a million years where I was employed. I accepted a position working for the Virginia Department of Corrections, as a rehabilitation counselor, in a prison! I did not have a criminal record, and I had not been convicted of a crime; therefore, I was qualified for the position. It is ironic that I went from being almost charged, convicted, and imprisoned for a crime that I did not commit, to working in a prison.

After working for years in law enforcement and arresting people, I now got to see what happens to the offenders after they have been committed to prison. I worked in the prison for less than a year before I was promoted and appointed to the position of probation and parole officer, which required an appointment by a circuit court judge. Several years later, I was promoted to senior probation and parole officer.

∞

CHAPTER 11: THE AUTHORITIES' BIG BREAK IN THE INVESTIGATION

Although the authorities were continuing their investigation, the next five years brought little that was new. In 1997, newly elected Fulton County District Attorney Paul L. Howard, Jr. began aggressively investigating Lita Sullivan's murder in cooperation with a major felony squad. In 1998, the authorities received their big break in the case when a Texas resident named Belinda Trahan came forward with information regarding Lita Sullivan's murder.

Ms. Trahan recognized Jim Sullivan on television as the man that she and a former boyfriend met in a Florida diner after Lita Sullivan had been murdered. Trahan told authorities that her ex-boyfriend, Phillip Anthony (Tony) Harwood, was paid $25,000 by Jim Sullivan to kill Lita Sullivan. Trahan told authorities that she dated Harwood in 1987 while living in North Carolina. For the first time, the authorities had the name of a suspect they could connect with the murder of Lita Sullivan.

Trahan told the authorities that she dated Harwood for three years and that Harwood met Jim Sullivan when he delivered furniture to the Palm Beach mansion in 1986. Harwood was living at that time in

Albemarle, North Carolina, and working for or contracted with North American Van Lines.

The authorities wasted no time in obtaining an indictment for Harwood, who was arrested on April 19, 1998 and brought to Atlanta. He supposedly told the authorities that he had been expecting them. Harwood was offered a plea deal by prosecutors in a move to finger Jim Sullivan. Harwood then provided the following information to the authorities.

He said that he had delivered a baby grand piano and some other items to Sullivan's Palm Beach mansion in November of 1986. At that time, according to Harwood, Sullivan told him that he was having a problem with his black wife, who was trying to take all of his money in a divorce proceeding. Sullivan supposedly asked Harwood if he knew of anyone who could take care of his problem. At some point, Harwood and Sullivan agreed on a figure of $25,000. Harwood either agreed to kill Lita himself or to hire someone to carry out the contract murder.

Harwood said that he returned to North Carolina and told Belinda Trahan about Sullivan's proposition. (Trahan claimed that she did not believe Harwood.) Harwood also said that he did not believe Sullivan was sincere until he received two cashiers or certified checks in the mail totaling $12,500. Harwood said that he initially thought about keeping the money without acting on the agreement, but added that he feared Sullivan might do something to him if he did not act as agreed. Harwood told the authorities that the contract hit was supposed to be carried out before Christmas of 1986.

Harwood also admitted to authorities that he was the shooter, but he later recanted his story and said that a bartender named John was the shooter. Harwood said that John and a stripper named Tracy Slye were involved in Lita's murder. Although Harwood eventually worked out a plea agreement with authorities in exchange for a twenty-year sentence (in lieu of a possible death sentence) he repeatedly flip-flopped in his story, and did not produce his accomplices. Rumor had it that he was possibly protecting someone, perhaps a family member.

I already stated that I do not know any of the subjects that the authorities previously questioned me about. I would also like to state that I do not know Phillip Anthony Harwood, Belinda Trahan, Tracey

Slye, John the bartender, Johnny Faircloth or any of Harwood's accomplices.

Finally, all of the pieces of the puzzle were put together, with the exception of Harwood's supposed two accomplices. The following sequence of events is a combination of information provided to the authorities by Harwood, information and evidence obtained by the authorities, and information resulting from my investigation:

On November 24, 1986, while Tony Harwood was working for North American Van Lines, he transported a baby grand piano and other items from Macon to Sullivan's Palm Beach mansion in Florida. Harwood stated that he remembered scratching Jim Sullivan's floor in the mansion as he was bringing in the piano. At some point, Jim Sullivan mentioned to him that he had a problem and wanted to know if Harwood knew of anyone who could help him with it. Sullivan said that his wife was trying to take him for everything that he had, and he was looking for someone to take care of his problem. Harwood stated that he took those words to mean, "kill her."

After further discussion, Harwood told Sullivan that he knew of someone, or that he could take care of the problem. Sullivan asked Harwood how much it would cost. Harwood came up with a figure of $25,000, which Sullivan agreed to pay. He gave Harwood his telephone numbers; Harwood gave Sullivan his address. Sullivan made it clear that he wanted the hit carried out before December 25, 1986, and Harwood agreed to carry out the hit before Christmas. Sullivan then gave Harwood the address of the townhouse in Buckhead, Atlanta. Harwood left the mansion and returned to his home near Albemarle, North Carolina.

Harwood told Belinda Trahan about Sullivan's proposition but she did not believe him. Harwood then received two checks totaling $12,500.

It is unclear if Harwood made an attempt on Lita's life before December 25, 1986. On January 13, 1987, Harwood and two accomplices drove to Atlanta from North Carolina, and one of them rang Lita Sullivan's doorbell and pounded on the door of her Buckhead townhouse sometime between 4:00 a.m. and 6:00 a.m.; however, Lita did not answer the door. Harwood and his two male accomplices checked into room 518 at the Howard Johnson's Motor Lodge in the Sandy Springs area of Atlanta on Roswell Road. (Harwood alternatively claimed at some point that he checked into the Howard Johnson's with a bartender named John and a stripper named Tracy Slye. However, none of the witnesses in the case mentioned a female, nor did the authorities indicate the presence of a female.)

Harwood called Sullivan to discuss his failed attempt and to tell Sullivan that Lita did not open the door. This must have brought up the question of whether or not Lita was at home or still living in the townhouse. Sullivan called me just after 7:00 a.m. and left a panicked message on my voicemail, stating that he urgently needed information about Lita's whereabouts and whether she was living with someone. When I returned his call, I told him that I did not know. Sullivan then placed the aforementioned two calls to attorney Bob Christenson, wanting to know if Christenson had seen any strange people or vehicles in the townhouse complex where Christenson and Lita Sullivan both lived. Sullivan also asked him if he heard any loud knocking on Lita's door early that morning, and he also asked Christenson for Lita's telephone number.

It is my theory that Jim Sullivan doubted whether Harwood and his accomplices had actually attempted to carry out the hit. I also think Sullivan wanted to know if Lita had temporarily moved out of the townhouse; that would explain the questions that he posed to me and Bob Christenson.

Harwood and his accomplices returned to North Carolina. Harwood told Trahan that he could not get Lita Sullivan to answer the door. Trahan, instead of going to the authorities with information about a plot to kill Lita Sullivan, suggested to Harwood that the way to get a lady to answer the door was to bring flowers.

And if that does not equal conspiracy, conspiracy does not exist.

So what did Harwood do? Exactly what Trahan suggested to him. On January 16, 1987, Harwood and his cohorts returned to Atlanta for a second attempt on Lita Sullivan's life.

Around 8:00 a.m. on January 16th, one of Harwood's accomplices purchased one dozen pink roses from Botany Bay Florist on Peachtree Road, not far from Lita Sullivan's townhouse. The florist stated that there were two men; one waited in the car while the other purchased the flowers. (Neither of the men fit Harwood's description.) Harwood's exact location at that point is unclear, but he was not far away. My theory is that he did not want to be seen by the florist for fear of being identified later. The florist, Randall Benson, told authorities that both of the men made him extremely nervous, and he felt that he was about to be robbed. Benson said that the two men seemed to be in a hurry, which made him even more nervous. If you recall, Benson had such a bad feeling about the two men that he only wired five of the twelve long-stemmed pink roses. Benson said that the men did not want a bag or a receipt.

The two men then met up with Harwood around 8:10 to 8:15 and gave him the box of roses. Bob Christenson saw a suspicious-looking man hurrying towards Lita's townhouse. Lita was upstairs in the townhouse preparing to go to the important property-settlement hearing scheduled for later that day regarding the validity of her postnuptial agreement. Lita was hoping that the postnuptial agreement would be ruled invalid that day; the voiding of the postnuptial agreement could have significantly increased Lita's entitlement in her divorce proceedings. Lita's close friend Poppy Finley Marable and her infant daughter Ingrid had spent the night and were also upstairs.

At approximately 8:20 a.m. Harwood rang Lita Sullivan's doorbell. Lita told Poppy that she would get the door. She walked downstairs and answered the door, greeting Tony Harwood by saying, "Good morning." Harwood handed Lita the white box containing the dozen pink roses and then fired two shots from a 9 mm automatic handgun. One of the rounds passed through the box of roses and struck Lita in the head. Lita lay mortally wounded on the marble foyer floor as Harwood fled on foot towards West Paces Ferry Road. Poppy heard the shots and hid in a bathroom with Ingrid after locking the door. Fearing that the gunman might come upstairs, she placed Ingrid on the floor of the closet.

Bob Christenson heard the shots and saw a man running from Lita's townhouse. He had to decide in a matter of seconds whether to chase the fleeing man or go to Lita's aid. He decided to rush to Lita's aid. Reluctant to open the door for fear of what lay behind, Christenson pushed the partially ajar door open. He found Lita lying face up on the foyer floor, clothed in a white bathrobe. A pool of blood had formed around her head. Christenson ran to the kitchen and dialed 911. He then went back to the foyer to comfort Lita. After the authorities arrived, Poppy emerged from the bathroom with Ingrid. Poppy asked the police officer if Lita was alive; the officer said that Lita was barely alive and that it did not look good. One of the first police officers on the scene held Lita's hand to comfort her, until the ambulance arrived. The officer said that Lita squeezed his hand, as if she were comforting him.

Poppy then hysterically called Lita's mother, JoAnn McClinton, and told her that Lita had been shot. Mrs. McClinton called her husband Emory. Mr. McClinton arrived at Lita's residence ahead of his wife. When Mrs. McClinton arrived, the paramedics were putting Lita into the ambulance. The McClintons followed the ambulance to Piedmont Hospital in separate cars. Soon after they arrived at the hospital, Lita was pronounced dead. She had died enroute to the hospital or shortly after arrival.

Harwood and his co-conspirators got on Interstate 85 and drove as far as a rest area in Suwanee, Georgia. Harwood called Sullivan approximately forty minutes after the contract murder, and greeted him by saying, "Merry Christmas." Perhaps the greeting was a reference to the date that Harwood agreed to have carried out the murder—Christmas 1986. It also informed Sullivan that Lita had been killed.

Many more details are covered in the Special Topic Section index in this book.

There are a few things that trouble me about Ms. Trahan. Why did she wait for more than ten years to come forth with this information, and what was her motivation? The reward money being offered? Trahan admitted to suggesting that Harwood buy flowers to get Lita to open her door. As Harwood's girlfriend in 1986 and 1987, it would seem likely that she took advantage of the money that Harwood received from Jim Sullivan. Trahan would also accompany Harwood to get the other half of the payment after Lita was murdered, and meet Jim Sullivan. If she was so innocent, why didn't she speak to the authorities at any time during these events?

According to law, it seems to me that Belinda Trahan could have been considered a conspirator or co-conspirator in the murder of Lita Sullivan. If it sounds as if I am more than agitated with Trahan, I am! If she had gone to the authorities and advised them of Harwood's plot to kill Lita, it is conceivable that Lita Sullivan would be alive today. If she had fingered Harwood before the contract murder was carried out, it would have led back to Jim Sullivan—not to mention that the authorities would have known that I was in no way involved in Jim Sullivan's plot to kill Lita Sullivan.

Did the authorities think about Trahan being a conspirator? The authorities investigated me for years because of Trahan. The authorities were so interested in what she had to say that they granted her immunity against prosecution. Why didn't the authorities at least charge her with conspiracy to commit murder and then work out a deal in exchange for her testimony against Harwood? It's possible she could have led the authorities to the other co-conspirators Harwood refused to finger in his plea deal. Just because a person goes to the authorities voluntarily with information regarding a crime that he or she had knowledge of and assisted with (advising someone to purchase flowers, in this case, constitutes planning) and knowledge of an impending crime, does not exonerate him or her from criminal liability.

After Trahan split from Harwood, she claimed that he repeatedly threatened to kill her. She stated that she lived in fear, hiding in a crawl space under her house for months with a loaded .357 magnum handgun. She stated that she was afraid that Harwood or Sullivan would hurt her.

∞

CHAPTER 12: JAMES VINCENT SULLIVAN CAPTURED IN THAILAND AND RETURNED TO THE UNITED STATES

On June 26, 1998, the authorities issued a five-count indictment against James Vincent Sullivan, charging him with murder, felony murder, aggravated assault (two counts), and burglary. But there was one major problem: Sullivan was out of the country. Jim Sullivan had moved to Faro Escondido, a luxurious condominium oceanfront resort in Costa Rica. He moved soon after District Attorney Paul Howard took office in 1997. Sullivan's attorney advised him of the indictment by telephone, and Sullivan agreed to return to the United States. However, he had other plans.

Sullivan drove to the airport in Panama City with two Costa Ricans (a brother and sister), leaving behind his home, his automobile, and his dog Coco. It was not until Sullivan arrived at the airport that he told his companions that he would not be returning. He gave them gas money to return to Costa Rica, headed to the terminal with his two suitcases, and flew to Caracas, Venezuela, and eventually ended up in Thailand. There had also been sightings of James Sullivan in the Cayman Islands, Guatemala, the Philippines, Ireland, and Switzerland.

Sullivan purchased a condominium in the Hua Hin condominium complex in the Springfield Beach resort area of Cha-Am, about a hundred miles south of Bangkok, for $128,000. He was living with Chongwattana Sriharoenmuang Reynolds, who was either his fourth wife or common-law wife.

The authorities did not know Sullivan's whereabouts, so they issued an international federal warrant for his arrest. In 2001, the FBI offered a $500,000 reward for information leading to his arrest and conviction. The authorities also took out an ad in *U.S.A. Today*. Sullivan was featured on *America's Most Wanted*. The authorities eventually received information that Sullivan was living in Thailand, and on July 2, 2002, he was arrested for the murder of Lita McClinton Sullivan. When he answered the door to his condominium, it was reported, he was in total shock and disbelief that the authorities had finally caught him.

On February 14, 2003, the McClintons had an opportunity to confront Phillip Anthony Harwood at his sentencing, where he received twenty years in prison for voluntary manslaughter. Emory McClinton Sr. spoke to Harwood and told him that he was not going to be forgiven for Lita's death because he worked out a deal with authorities. JoAnn McClinton prepared a written statement, saying that her family continued to suffer the loss of Lita, even though many years had passed since her death.

Initially, Sullivan had agreed to waive extradition to the United States, but later changed his mind and decided to fight extradition. In 2003, a Thai court ruled that Sullivan should be returned to the United States to face trial for the murder of Lita McClinton Sullivan. Sullivan appealed the decision to the court of appeals. In 2004, the court of appeals upheld the lower court's decision. Jim Sullivan had dual citizenship in the United States and in Ireland. During that time, Ireland would not extradite a person facing the death penalty. Sullivan attempted to use his Irish citizenship to avoid being returned to the United States, but his plan failed. On March 26, 2004, after spending nearly two years in a Thai jail he was returned to the United States to face trial for Lita's murder.

HIDDEN ASSETS

Emory and JoAnn McClinton had obtained a $4 million judgment against Jim Sullivan in a Florida civil court case, but locating his money was a challenge. Sullivan traveled to many countries after he sold the Palm Beach mansion and, while traveling, he began hiding his assets. He hid his assets so well that the McClintons would search for years in an attempt to locate Sullivan's money.

I remembered what Jim Sullivan had said the evening we had dinner in Atlanta with regard to paying in cash: "If you use cash, it cannot be traced." At the time I thought the statement was peculiar; but perhaps it makes sense now.

Jim sold the liquor distributorship for $5 million. He also sold the Palm Beach mansion for $3.2 million, and sold the townhouse. If you deduct the purchase price of the mansion, and other miscellaneous deductions, that could possibly leave $5.5 million. It is also possible that he had additional assets, depending on what he netted from the sale of the townhouse.

What happened to Jim's assets? Some of what you are about to read is based on fact as discovered by the authorities, some is based on research, and some is based on my own speculative theory.

When Jim realized that the authorities were aggressively investigating him for his role in Lita's murder, he began to protect his assets. One of the first things he did was sell the mansion in Palm Beach. Now, what did he do with the profits from the sale? There are countries that have laws designed to protect foreign assets as well as the identity of the individual investing there. Three of these countries, the Philippines, the Grand Cayman Islands (overseas territory of Great Britain), and Switzerland, happen to be countries where Jim was supposedly seen during his global trek. (I remember that Jim had occasionally gone scuba diving in the Cayman Islands.)

Although some countries have tightened the reins on foreign deposits, the aforementioned countries still have laws that are much more liberal than those of the United States. Some foreign countries have laws designed to protect the identity of the depositors and make it difficult to locate the assets and/or trace the deposit back to the owner.

Jim's strategy was probably, first, to live in a country that would not extradite to the United States for a death penalty case, and second, to conceal his investments in that country. As we are aware, that is not what happened, at least not the first part. Jim probably started protecting some of his assets soon after Lita was murdered.

There are a number of ways to hide assets. The more layered the transactions are, the more difficult it becomes to locate or identify the funds. To avoid leaving a global trail, a courier can be used to make the first foreign deposit of funds. This would make it hard to trace the funds back to an individual in the United States. A wire transfer would be too easy to identify. How do you put funds in a foreign account that will be accessible to you, but which is not in your name? One of the most popular ways is to set up multiple dummy corporations and trusts to which you have access by way of ownership.

Jim Sullivan set up a dummy corporation in the British West Indies called Nicola Resources. The funds were then placed in a new trust called Walpart. The trust was managed by an attorney from Liechtenstein. Jim would then have the money electronically wired to him. One of the wire transfers was for $19,000, to Thailand. Jim used the funds to purchase a BMW.

Another way to hide assets is to set up a revocable trust and use part of your name or your initials. This makes it more difficult to identify the owner or locate the funds. Other methods to hide assets are to convert funds to cash and stash the funds in different locations, frequently change banks, purchase bearer bonds, use a safe-deposit box, and put the funds in someone else's name—or use a combinations of these methods. The person trying to hide assets would probably use multiple financial institutions in foreign countries; that way, if one of the institutions is identified, not all of the hidden assets would be recovered or forfeited.

There are probably many other ways to hide assets, based on individual situations. The person hiding the assets always attempts to stay one step ahead of the person trying to identify or locate the assets.

The irony of this whole case is, if Jim Sullivan had given Lita half of his assets (at the time, approximately $2.75 million), and kept the Palm Beach mansion, he would still be a wealthy individual. The Palm Beach mansion sold for approximately $13 million, six years after it was sold by Sullivan. Today, the mansion is probably worth $17 million. The current annual property taxes on the mansion are approximately $253,000. Also, how much did Sullivan pay in legal fees?

* * *

SULLIVAN RETURNED TO THE UNITED STATES

After Sullivan was returned to Atlanta, there were numerous hearings and challenges made by his defense team. Sullivan's team—Ed Garland, Don Samuel, and Josh Moore—filed a petition to have the court throw out the indictments against him, based on double jeopardy; the lawyers contended that the 1992 federal murder for hire through interstate commerce trial exempted Sullivan from being tried for murder in a state court. But in 2005 the Supreme Court of Georgia ruled out double jeopardy stemming from the 1992 federal trial.

District Attorney Paul Howard announced that he was seeking the death penalty in the case. The prosecution's team consisted of Clinton (Clint) Rucker, Sheila Ross, Anna Green, and Kellie Hill. The prosecution worked day and night to prepare for what would possibly be the trial of the century. Trying a case after nearly twenty years had passed would definitely be a challenge, especially when up against Sullivan's high-powered defense team.

The estate of Lita Sullivan attempted to place a lien on Sullivan's defense funds, alleging that those funds were under a court-ordered judgment in a civil suit. Sullivan's defense team countered the claim by arguing that in accordance with Sullivan's constitutional rights, he had the right to hire lawyers for representation, just as people with debt are allowed to continue spending.

The authorities also had the body of Frank Bienet exhumed (Bienet was Sullivan's uncle who initially owned Sullivan's liquor distributorship) due to the suspicion that foul play may have been involved in his death; however, the autopsy did not reveal any evidence of this.

Sullivan appeared before Superior Court Judge John J. Goger and pleaded not guilty to all five counts of the indictment.

During a pre-trial hearing, Sullivan's defense team challenged statements and testimony given by Belinda Trahan. Trahan's credibility was challenged because she initially stated that after reviewing photographs, she was only forty percent sure of Sullivan's identity.

The defense team also challenged the testimony and credibility of Tony Harwood. Harwood alleged that he had been threatened by the prosecution. He alleged that the prosecution told him that he would face the death penalty if he did not testify against Sullivan. The prosecution denied the allegations, and Judge Goger ruled that both Trahan and Harwood would be permitted to testify during Sullivan's trial.

∞

CHAPTER 13:
THE STATE MURDER TRIAL

Nearly two years after Jim Sullivan was extradited to the United States, his trial was finally put on the court calendar. The delays were due to the many pre-trial hearings and challenges by Sullivan's defense team. Jury selection began on January 5, 2006, from a pool of approximately 450 prospective jurors. The final result of the jury selection was thirteen women and three men, which included four alternates. The trial was scheduled to begin on February 28, and was expected to run approximately four weeks. The judge ordered the jurors to be sequestered for the duration of the trial.

In January of 2006, I received a telephone call from Fulton County Senior Assistant District Attorney Clint Rucker advising me that I would be subpoenaed to testify for the prosecution. Rucker and investigator Frederick Hall traveled to Virginia to meet with me and discuss the upcoming trial. I was served with the subpoena and advised that I would be scheduled to testify during the second week of the trial.

TRIAL DAY ONE: TUESDAY, FEBRUARY 28, 2006

During their opening statements, Sullivan's defense team alleged that the prosecution was about to present a circumstantial case and that their key witnesses were either habitual liars or lacked credibility. The defense also claimed that jailhouse liars who were trying to get a better deal on their sentences were out to frame Jim Sullivan. Don Samuel claimed that Sullivan did not flee the United States, because he left before any arrest warrant was issued. (He did not elaborate on the fact that Sullivan fled Costa Rica after he learned of his murder indictment.) The defense then advised the jury that the prosecution did not have any physical evidence linking Jim Sullivan to Lita Sullivan's death.

The prosecution, in its opening statements, said that Sullivan was a greedy philanderer who was willing to murder his wife to keep his millions. ADA Sheila Ross went on to explain how Sullivan would profit from Lita's death. The prosecution then said that Sullivan opted to flee halfway around the world to avoid facing prosecution for Lita's death. The prosecution also reminded the jury that Harwood had fired shots at Lita Sullivan, striking her in the head and killing her.

JoAnn McClinton took the stand and testified that Lita felt that Jim Sullivan was trying to kill her, and referred to the loud knocking on the Buckhead townhouse door just three days before Lita was murdered.

Lita's neighbor, Bob Christenson, testified that he was taking out his trash when he observed Harwood hurrying to Lita's townhouse door on the morning of January 16, 1987, with a white box in his hand. He then testified that he heard the two shots and observed Harwood running from the townhouse, without the box he had been carrying. He told the court that he ran to Lita's aid and found her mortally wounded; the box of pink roses lying beside her. He went on to relate how he had dialed 911 and placed a towel under Lita's head in an attempt to stop the bleeding.

Christenson also testified about the telephone calls from Sullivan on January 13, 1987, inquiring about suspicious people, a green vehicle, and whether he heard loud knocking on Lita's door. He testified that he had not spoken to Sullivan for over a year before the January 13 call. Christenson also made a positive identification of Harwood from photographs, thus placing Harwood at the murder scene. (Another neighbor had previously told authorities that they saw Harwood running out of the Coaches complex and that they almost struck him with their car.)

The prosecution then questioned Poppy Marable, who had spent the night at the townhouse with her three-year-old daughter. Ms. Marable, who was upstairs at the time the murder occurred, testified that she heard the doorbell ring and that Lita went downstairs to answer the door. She said that she heard Lita say, "Good morning," and then heard three shots—"Pow, pow, pow"—and that she then heard a thump, which was Lita hitting the foyer floor.

Defense attorney Josh Moore questioned Ms. Marable about Lita's friend Bob Daniels, who had supposedly threatened to kill Lita days before her murder. Marable stated that Daniels and Lita were good friends and that he had attended Lita Sullivan's memorial service.

Retired judge Ed Wheeler, a former friend and associate of Sullivan's, testified that Sullivan stated that he would employ "scorched-earth tactics" in pursuing his divorce. Judge Wheeler testified that he took that to mean that Sullivan was suggesting that if he (Sullivan) could not have his assets, Lita could not have them, either. Wheeler testified that he told Jim Sullivan, as a friend, that he thought Lita Sullivan would prevail in their divorce proceedings.

The florist Randal Benson, who sold the pink roses, was now deceased, but his trial testimony from 1992, his deposition, and his statements were introduced into evidence.

TRIAL DAY TWO: WEDNESDAY, MARCH 1, 2006

Lita Sullivan's former divorce attorney, Richard Schiffman, testified that Jim Sullivan could have lost $1 million of his assets if Lita had prevailed in her divorce case. Schiffman said that he was certain that Judge Daniel would have voided the postnuptial agreement that gave Lita only $2,500 per month for three years, and other assets. Schiffman also testified that Lita's legal fees had totaled approximately $50,000 and that Sullivan's legal fees were nearly $100,000.

Schiffman told the court that the initial temporary alimony was set at $7,000 per month and that Jim Sullivan refused to pay as ordered by Judge Daniel. The temporary alimony was then reduced to $2,500 per month as requested by Sullivan's divorce lawyer. Schiffman added that Sullivan even refused to pay the $2,500 and was fined $15,000 by Judge Daniel. During that time, Sullivan was receiving over $20,000 per month in installment payments from the sale of his liquor distributorship, Crown Beverages.

The prosecution questioned Schiffman about Jim Sullivan's liability to Lita Sullivan after she was murdered. Schiffman said that Jim Sullivan owed nothing more after Lita's death, meaning that all liability to the deceased ended with their death. He also testified that he received a call from Sullivan's attorney after Lita Sullivan's death and was advised that Jim did not want Lita's family to remove anything from the Buckhead townhouse. He said that he told Jim Sullivan's attorney that he was not going to call the McClintons on the day that their daughter was killed and ask them not to remove furniture or other items from the townhouse. Schiffman added that the Sullivan divorce was the most difficult case that he had handled in his twenty-five years as an attorney.

Schiffman testified that he had been optimistic about how Judge Daniel was going to rule regarding the validity of the post-nuptial agreement; however, under cross-examination he stated that he did not know how Judge Daniel would have ruled.

A long-time friend and former neighbor of Lita Sullivan from Macon, Jan Marlow Allen, testified that Lita told her about the early-morning pounding on her townhouse door on January 13, 1987. Ms. Allen testified that Lita told her that a tall white man with a short-brimmed hat had banged on her door at that time.

The prosecution was laying its foundation for Jim Sullivan's motive to have Lita Sullivan killed, which was to keep all of his assets and not share anything with his estranged wife. The prosecution also introduced evidence which showed that Jim Sullivan needed Lita Sullivan's signature to obtain a mortgage to pay off a balloon note on the Palm Beach mansion. Howard Steklof, a bank manager from Boca Raton, Florida, testified that he advised Sullivan that if he were married, his wife's signature would be required on the approximately $900,000 loan that he was seeking. He further testified that soon after Lita Sullivan's death he received a call from Jim Sullivan, who said that his wife was dead and that he wanted to proceed with the loan request. Jim Sullivan never mentioned to Steklof that Lita was murdered; he merely produced Lita's death certificate. Two months later, Sullivan received a loan of $960,000.

A video company representative testified that Sullivan's divorce attorney called on January 9, 1987, to schedule a videotaping of the contents of the Buckhead townhouse. The representative also said that Sullivan's attorney called him back on January 15, 1987 and cancelled the scheduled videotaping. The next morning, Lita Sullivan was murdered.

Sullivan's defense team attempted to counter the allegations of the prosecution by saying that Sullivan had no reason to believe that Judge Daniel was not going to rule in his favor; therefore, he would have had no motive to kill Lita Sullivan.

ADA Sheila Ross then allowed Lita's parents to leave the courtroom before she showed the jury the bloody crime scene photographs and the blood-stained robe that Lita was wearing the day she was murdered. The prosecution team used numerous large posters and a big screen monitor to present illustrations and evidence to the jury.

Welcome Harris of the Atlanta Police Department (now Major Harris), who was one of the initial lead investigators working the Lita Sullivan murder case, testified that Jim Sullivan remained a suspect in Lita's murder even after his 1992 acquittal in the federal murder trial.

A representative from the Southern Bell Telephone Company testified that a one-minute collect telephone call was made from a Suwanee, Georgia, rest area off Interstate 85, to Sullivan's mansion in Palm Beach on January 16, 1987. The call was made approximately 40-45 minutes after Lita Sullivan was murdered. Interstate 85, going north from Atlanta, is a route that can be taken to Albemarle, North

Carolina, where Tony Harwood lived at the time of Lita Sullivan's murder.

TRIAL DAY THREE: THURSDAY, MARCH 2, 2006

Authorities presented evidence pertaining to long distance telephone calls made to and from the Howard Johnson's Motor Lodge located in Sandy Springs on Roswell Road in metropolitan Atlanta. One of the three registered guests who checked in to room 518 of the motel on January 13, 1987 as Johnny Furr, turned out to be none other than Phillip Anthony Harwood, the triggerman. Handwriting expert Arthur Anthony of the GBI authenticated Harwood's handwriting as the same as the handwriting of "Johnny Furr." Harwood was also known to have used this alias name on other occasions. The Howard Johnson's records showed that the trio paid cash for the $77.00 room. Former FBI Special Agent John Kingston testified that Harwood placed a telephone call from the Howard Johnson's at 7:44 a.m., just twenty minutes after checking in to the motel.

That same day, Sullivan made several telephone calls from his Palm Beach mansion, including calls to Bob Christenson and to me. Sullivan was desperately trying to gather information on Lita Sullivan. Sullivan then made a telephone call to room 518 at the Howard Johnson's at approximately 10:33 a.m. The prosecution team was trying to make a connection between the telephone calls and the failed attempt to murder Lita Sullivan in the early morning hours of January 13th.

Telephone records from Concord, North Carolina, confirmed that Harwood made at least two telephone calls from his residence in Mount Pleasant, North Carolina, to Jim Sullivan in Palm Beach, Florida. The calls were made on June 19, 1987, and July 1, 1987. Sullivan's defense team claimed that the telephone calls were related to their client resolving some damaged-furniture issues.

Forensic accountant Joseph Miller testified that Sullivan had $7.9 million in assets at the time of Lita's murder, which included the Palm Beach mansion, the Buckhead townhouse in Atlanta, two Mercedes-Benzes, a Rolls-Royce, and a classic 1957 Thunderbird automobile. He also testified that Sullivan had liabilities totaling $2.4 million, some of which included seven mortgages on his real estate properties. Sullivan's net worth was established at $5.5 million.

FBI Special Agent Todd Letcher testified that Sullivan maintained a detailed daily journal but failed to make an entry regarding Lita's death or her memorial service. Instead, there were several entries regarding his soon-to-be third wife, Suki Rogers. The prosecution attempted to introduce one of Sullivan's journal entries that read, "buy flowers," in an attempt to connect it to the pink roses purchased by one of Harwood's co-conspirators. The journal entry was made just days before Lita's murder, but Judge Goger ruled it inadmissible.

Agent Letcher was questioned about potential suspects identified earlier in the investigation. He testified that Thomas Bruce Henley was a suspect and that florist Randall Benson said that Henley "looked like the driver of the car," referring to the white Toyota driven by one of Harwood's accomplices. Henley was arrested based on an elaborate, fabricated story by Johnny Austin Turner that supposedly also linked me to Lita Sullivan's murder. Henley was later released due to lack of evidence and because he had an alibi.

Letcher also testified that the florist picked a person named Johnny Faircloth from a photo line-up, identifying him as being the person that bought the pink roses. Faircloth was not considered a suspect (incidentally, he died three months after Lita was murdered). Letcher testified under cross-examination that he had become suspicious of me after Poppy Marable and Lita Sullivan discovered the wiretapping device in the basement of my wife's and my residence in 1986. Sullivan's attorney Don Samuel suggested that I had motive to kill Lita Sullivan after she prosecuted me for recording her conversations. Samuel also mentioned that I had failed a polygraph test and that I would not testify without immunity during Sullivan's first trial. The jury was not present when Samuel made the statement about the polygraph test and the immunity.

That afternoon, I received a call from investigator Frederick Hall of the Fulton County DA's office, who wanted to know if I could fly from Virginia to Atlanta that afternoon. It was apparent that the prosecution wanted to clear up some allegation made by the defense team. I told Hall that it would be impossible for me to get to Atlanta before the judge recessed for the day, and he said he would call me back. Later in the day, he called to say that I was not needed at that time. He also told me that there was a possibility that I would not have to testify at any time during the trial. The prosecution and defense could stipulate how I would testify, therefore making it unnecessary for me to appear in court. My testimony from Sullivan's 1992 Federal trial was also available to the prosecution and the defense.

TRIAL DAY FOUR: FRIDAY, MARCH 3, 2006

During this court session, the prosecution presented testimony from Belinda Trahan, Harwood's former girlfriend. ADA Clint Rucker asked Ms. Trahan if she could identify James Sullivan, and she said, "He's right there," as she pointed to Sullivan seated at the defense table. Trahan then added, "He can't even make eye contact." Trahan testified that she had been dating Harwood in the late 1980s and that she had lived with him in a trailer located on Harwood's parents' property in Albemarle, North Carolina. Harwood's parents lived in a house also located on the property.

Trahan went on to say that Harwood was acting strange after he returned from a North American Van Lines moving job in Georgia and Florida. She said that Harwood told her that he had met someone in Florida who wanted to get rid of his wife. Trahan said that she did not believe Harwood and that she thought he had been to a strip club and was seeing another woman.

Trahan then testified that Harwood returned from Atlanta in January of 1987 and told her he had not been able to get Lita Sullivan to open her door. She repeated that everyone knows that flowers will get a woman to open the door. Harwood returned to Atlanta three days later and had one of his accomplices buy the pink roses. Trahan stated that Harwood returned to North Carolina and advised her that the job was done.

Trahan had originally told the authorities that she took a ride with Harwood to meet with Sullivan two or three days after Lita Sullivan was murdered. In court, she testified that she rode with Harwood to meet with Sullivan two to three *weeks* after Lita Sullivan's murder. She stated that she rode in the back seat of Harwood's car to meet with Jim Sullivan in a diner. She said that she and Harwood walked into the diner and approached the booth where Sullivan was sitting. She said Sullivan looked at her and asked Harwood, "What's she doing here?" She and Harwood took a seat at the booth opposite Sullivan and Harwood said, "She's okay."

According to Trahan's testimony, Sullivan appeared to be very upset by her presence. She said that she looked out the window to avoid making eye contact with him. She added that she looked back toward the table when Sullivan slid a newspaper toward Harwood and said she also noticed that Sullivan's fingernails were manicured. She said Sullivan then got up and walked out of the diner and that she and Harwood waited for a brief period before they left the diner.

After she and Harwood left the diner and got back into his car, Harwood opened the newspaper, which had concealed an envelope. Trahan testified that Harwood opened the envelope and found that it was filled with cash, presumably $12,500, which would represent the balance of the money promised to him by Sullivan, but that he did not count it. Trahan testified that she did see the money but could not determine how much money was in the envelope. (The prosecution had set up a mock booth for Trahan to demonstrate what transpired at the diner.)

Trahan then testified that while she soon ended her three-year relationship with Harwood, troubled times followed. She said that she moved to Texas and that Harwood began threatening to harm her and her son if she did not stay in a relationship with him. She said that Harwood would show up at her house unannounced and that she maintained a sexual relationship with him in order to avoid being harmed by him. In addition to the threats, she also found a black rose on her doorstep and thought that Harwood had someone watching her.

She stated that she lived in fear and that Harwood had threatened to kill her and then kill himself.

Under cross-examination, Sullivan's attorney Ed Garland questioned Ms. Trahan for nearly an hour and a half. Trahan testified that she could not remember many of the details regarding the trip that she took with Harwood to meet Sullivan and that she could not even remember how long they traveled or the state where the diner was located. Garland implied that Trahan's memory had faded, and she agreed.

After Trahan had reported Harwood to the authorities regarding Lita Sullivan's murder, she recorded some of her subsequent conversations with him, as requested by them. During one of the conversations, Harwood mentioned that he had given Trahan some of the money that he had received from Jim Sullivan, and that Trahan had been present when he opened a bank account and deposited some of the money. Trahan testified that she could not remember being at a bank with Harwood.

Next to testify was Sullivan's third wife, Suki Sullivan, who married Jim eight months after Lita's murder. Jim Sullivan had been dating Suki when Lita was murdered. Suki Sullivan testified that Jim had called her hours after Lita's death and told her that Lita's death was good for them. Suki testified that Jim had complained about having to share his estate with Lita and that he had tried to get the divorce proceedings moved from Georgia to Florida. She further testified that Sullivan told her that Lita would have an advantage by having the divorce case heard in Atlanta, because she was black. She said that her husband did not grieve after Lita was murdered.

Suki Sullivan had previously testified against Jim Sullivan during their divorce proceedings in 1990 and at his federal trial in 1992. During both court appearances, she testified that Jim had admitted to her that he had arranged to have Lita Sullivan killed. But for some reason, the prosecution elected not to question Suki Sullivan regarding her prior testimony of Jim Sullivan's admission.

A firearms expert, formerly with the GBI, testified that the gunman who killed Lita Sullivan first handed her the box of roses and then shot her. He also testified that one of the bullets passed through the box of roses as Lita and the gunman stood in the foyer of her townhouse. The prosecution used the expert to substantiate its charge of burglary against Sullivan. The fact that the gunman entered the premises of the townhouse and then killed Lita Sullivan confirmed the burglary charge.

TRIAL DAY FIVE: MONDAY, MARCH 6, 2006

After Belinda Trahan placed Harwood with Sullivan, it was now time for Harwood to take the stand. Harwood's testimony would be a challenge for the authorities, because he changed his story when he came before the jury.

The prosecution began by questioning Harwood regarding his former association with James Sullivan. Harwood repeated for the jury what he had already told the authorities, but with some changes. Harwood testified that he first met James Sullivan in November of 1986 when he was delivering a piano and items of furniture to Sullivan's Palm Beach mansion. The furnishings were being transported from Macon, Georgia, where Sullivan had previously resided. ADA Rucker asked Harwood to get up and face the jury and act out his conversation with Sullivan.

Harwood stood up and began talking to the jury as if he were James Sullivan. He said, "I've got this wife in Atlanta and she's just trying to take everything I've got. Do you know anyone that could possibly take care of my problem for me?" While Harwood was addressing the jury, he was standing next to a poster-sized picture of Lita Sullivan. Harwood then returned to his seat in the witness box and continued his testimony.

Harwood admitted to telling Sullivan that he could help him for a $25,000 payment, but he testified that he did not believe Sullivan—he felt that Sullivan was jiving or BS'ing him. ADA Rucker then asked Harwood when he began to believe Sullivan. Harwood said that he began to believe Sullivan when he received checks in the mail totaling $12,500, representing the down payment for the contract murder. Harwood then testified that he asked himself, "What do I do now?"

He said that he felt obligated to do something for fear of retaliation from Sullivan if, having received the money, he did not act.

At this point, Harwood's testimony changed dramatically from what he had initially stated to authorities and which was part of his plea agreement. Harwood said that he contacted a stripper named Tracy Slye, who put him in contact with a bartender named John (no last name). Harwood said that he, Tracy Slye, and John drove to Atlanta from North Carolina on January 13, 1987, and that he and John knocked on Lita Sullivan's townhouse door and rang the doorbell very early in the morning. Harwood claimed that he was going to warn Lita Sullivan of her estranged husband's intentions. He also testified that he was possibly going to ask Lita Sullivan if she wanted to place a hit on James Sullivan. Harwood further claimed that he never intended for Lita Sullivan to be harmed.

ADA Rucker then asked Harwood why he didn't attempt to contact Lita Sullivan by telephone or other means to warn her of the contract placed on her by Sullivan. Harwood testified that he did not think of it. He said that Lita Sullivan did not answer the door and that he and John returned to Atlanta on January 16, 1987.

Harwood went on to say that he purchased the flowers because Sullivan had told him that Lita adored roses. Harwood said that he gave them to John and then waited in the car while John took the roses to Lita's door and rang the doorbell. He stated that he heard two shots and that John then came running out of the townhouse complex to the car. He said he was shocked when he saw John running back to the car with blood splattered all over his face. He again claimed that he did not intend for Lita Sullivan to be killed. During the trial Harwood repeatedly stated that he did not kill Lita Sullivan.

It appeared as if Harwood was trying to convince the jury and the courtroom audience that he had been coerced by the authorities into admitting that he killed Lita Sullivan. He had previously stated that the prosecution told him that if he did not admit to killing Lita Sullivan, and did not admit being hired by James Sullivan to kill her, he could face the death penalty. Was Harwood perhaps trying to lay the groundwork to have his conviction overturned? ADA Rucker later said that Harwood was denying the fact that he was the shooter in an attempt to get his sentence reduced.

ADA Rucker made a bold attempt to get Harwood to admit in open court that he killed Lita Sullivan. Harwood's admission would give the prosecution an airtight case. Rucker asked Harwood if he killed Lita Sullivan. Harwood paused and then responded, "No." Rucker then asked Harwood to face the jury and state that he did not shoot and kill Lita Sullivan. Harwood turned to the jury and said, "I did not shoot and kill Lita Sullivan." This was a very tricky time for the prosecution. Harwood's continued denial could have brought into question the credibility of one of the prosecution's main witnesses, thereby raising doubt in the minds of the jurors. Although Harwood did not really have credibility to begin with, the prosecution was forced to use him as a witness. When the prosecution worked out a plea agreement with Harwood, they probably did not anticipate that he would deny killing Lita during the trial.

Rucker then asked Harwood about the collect telephone call made from the rest area in Suwanee, Georgia, approximately forty minutes after Lita was murdered. Harwood testified that he did call James Sullivan and that he (Harwood) said, "Merry Christmas," referring to the job being done. Harwood stated that James Sullivan responded by saying, "I understand."

Harwood's testimony also differed from Belinda Trahan's testimony regarding the meeting with Sullivan in the diner. Harwood stated that he and Trahan drove to a diner in Florida in August of 1987 and that they were already seated at a booth when Sullivan walked in and that he had observed Sullivan driving up to the diner in a green Volvo. Harwood said that he stood up to greet Sullivan, but that Sullivan continued walking past him. Harwood said that he went to the men's room, and when he returned Sullivan was sitting at the booth with Ms. Trahan, directly across from her. Harwood made no mention of Sullivan asking, "What is she doing here?" as alleged by Trahan in her testimony. Harwood also stated that Sullivan did not have anything in his hand—no newspaper or envelope—again contradicting Trahan's telling of events. Harwood said that he told Sullivan that they needed to talk and that he and Sullivan walked into the men's room, and that was where the final payment was made—not at the booth as claimed by Trahan.

Rucker then asked Harwood to identify the person that paid him to kill Lita Sullivan, and he looked directly at James Sullivan and pointed towards him. ADA Rucker asked Harwood why he hadn't come forward to tell the authorities that James Sullivan paid him to kill his wife. Harwood replied that he was afraid.

TRIAL DAY SIX: TUESDAY, MARCH 7, 2006

When the time came for the defense team to cross-examine Harwood, to the surprise of many, they declined. The conflicts in testimony between Trahan and Harwood almost certainly concerned the prosecution and were probably seen as favorable by the defense. I guess for the defense team, the pros of not questioning Harwood outweighed the cons. Would their strategy work?

The prosecution presented forensic evidence and testimony from the Fulton County Medical Examiner's Office. Chief Medical Examiner Randy Hazlick testified that the 9mm bullet that struck Lita Sullivan in the head did not hit her brain stem; therefore, her death was not instant. He testified that Lita Sullivan died of massive hemorrhaging within one hour after she was shot.

Retired GBI agent John Lang testified that when Harwood was arrested in Albemarle, North Carolina, he said, "I've been waiting for you guys for a long time."

In an effort to convince the jury that Jim Sullivan took flight to avoid arrest and prosecution and was not merely on an extended vacation, the prosecution team chronologically mapped out Sullivan's worldwide travel. They pointed out that Sullivan left Costa Rica so abruptly that he left behind many of his belongings, and even his dog Coco. The Costa Rican couple that rode with Sullivan to the airport in Panama testified that he drove fast and recklessly.

The defense again countered the prosecution's claim of Sullivan's flight from prosecution by alleging that Sullivan's world travels were an attempt to avoid the media.

After presenting evidence of Sullivan's global trek, the prosecution rested its case. Defense attorney Josh Moore made a motion to the court for a direct verdict of acquittal, but this was denied by Judge Goger.

TRIAL DAY SEVEN: WEDNESDAY, MARCH 8, 2006

The defense team called only two witnesses to testify. Tracy Slye, the former stripper who had previously dated one of Harwood's jail mates, testified remotely from Texas. Ms. Slye had previously lived in North Carolina but was currently living in Texas. She has a serious respiratory condition and uses a breathing machine, and was unable to travel to Atlanta for the trial.

Slye testified that she met Harwood in the 1980s and that she knew him through a former boyfriend. She stated that her former boyfriend and Harwood had served time in jail together when they were teenagers or in their early twenties. Defense attorney Samuel questioned Slye in an effort to discredit Harwood's testimony.

Slye testified that Harwood did in fact appear at a bar in North Carolina called the Palace, where she worked as a bartender and dancer. She said that they spoke only briefly. Slye denied talking to Harwood about arranging the murder of Lita Sullivan. She denied having any knowledge related to the death of Lita Sullivan. She denied traveling to Atlanta with Harwood and "John" and denied having any knowledge of Harwood's supposed attempt to warn Lita Sullivan of the planned murder or to call off the murder. Slye said that she did not see Harwood again after talking with him in the Palace. She said that she had seen Harwood's picture on *America's Most Wanted* in 1998, after he had been arrested for the murder of Lita Sullivan.

The next witness called by the defense was a friend and former attorney of James Sullivan. John Taylor testified that he had advised Jim Sullivan not to attend Lita Sullivan's memorial service because of how

Lita's parents, the McClintons, might respond to his presence. Taylor stated that because of the animosity between Sullivan and the McClintons, they would not have wanted him there. Taylor also added that Sullivan offered to help pay for the funeral services but that no assistance was requested from Lita's parents.

Taylor testified that he and another attorney made the decision to cancel the scheduled videotaping of the Buckhead townhouse contents, just one day before Lita was murdered. He said that Sullivan did not have any input in the decision to cancel the videotaping. Taylor stated that he felt that the videotaping could possibly have had a negative, rather than positive impact during a divorce jury trial.

ADA Ross questioned Taylor about whether or not he advised Jim Sullivan not to send flowers for Lita's memorial services or not to send a sympathy card, or not to call Lita's parents to express his condolences. Taylor replied that he did not advise Jim Sullivan *not* to do any of those things.

Taylor testified that he did not tell Lita Sullivan's divorce attorney, Rick Schiffman, to tell the McClintons not to take any contents from the Buckhead townhouse. Taylor said that he was concerned about securing the townhouse, and in no way directed his comments toward Lita's parents.

After John Taylor finished testifying, the defense rested its case.

Judge Goger instructed the jury to leave the courtroom so that he could speak with James Sullivan. The judge asked Sullivan if he wanted to testify on his own behalf. Sullivan conferred with his attorney, then declined to testify. Judge Goger then asked Sullivan if there was any doubt in his mind whether or not he wanted to testify; Sullivan again declined. Judge Goger dismissed the jury for the day.

TRIAL DAY EIGHT: THURSDAY, MARCH 9, 2006

ADA Clint Rucker delivered an extremely powerful closing argument. In his remarks, he acknowledged that while there were many circumstantial aspects to the case, the circumstantial evidence could not be disputed. An example he gave was the telephone calls made on January 13, 1987, between Sullivan's Palm Beach mansion and room 518 of the Howard Johnson's motel. Rucker said that the phone calls were not strange or a coincidence, but were evidence. He then exhorted the jurors to give Sullivan what he deserved— a verdict of guilty. Rucker reminded the jury of the handwriting analysis that matched Harwood's handwriting to the handwriting on the motel's registration form. He elaborated on the telephone call from the rest area off I-85 and he reminded the jury of the chilling message that Harwood delivered to James Sullivan: "Merry Christmas."

Rucker referred to James Sullivan as an assassin who was responsible for murdering his estranged wife nearly twenty years before. He pointed out that Sullivan's motivation was money, money that he did not want to share with his wife, Lita. He again stated that the evidence was indisputable: James Sullivan paid Phillip Anthony Harwood $25,000 to kill Lita Sullivan, and the motive was greed.

Rucker tried to downplay the fact that the prosecution's own witness, Anthony Harwood, had to be impeached because he changed his testimony when he denied killing Lita Sullivan. Rucker pounded his fist on the wooden railing that separated the jurors from the courtroom as he passionately said, "It really doesn't matter what Tony Harwood says. It is the mere existence of Tony Harwood that gives the state enough to prove this case beyond a reasonable doubt."

ADA Rucker had a doorbell set up in the courtroom, and he rang the doorbell twice, and then said, "The doorbell rings loud. It rings loud and clear, and in this case it rings true. This man right here—right here!—he is responsible for the assassination of Lita."

Rucker then added, "Even though he did not pull the trigger himself, even though he was lying in bed with his feet propped up, probably drinking some coffee, reading the newspaper, waiting to get the phone call from Tony Harwood, he is still guilty, just as if he pulled the trigger himself."

Now it was the defense team's turn to try to convince the jury that James Vincent Sullivan was not responsible for causing the death of Lita McClinton Sullivan. The defense focused on the prosecution's mostly circumstantial case and the credibility (or lack thereof) of the prosecution's key witnesses, Belinda Trahan and Tony Harwood.

Sullivan's attorney Ed Garland approached the jury and said that if they had any doubt about Harwood's testimony, that would be enough to find Sullivan not guilty. Garland also made reference to Harwood lying every time his lips were moving. Garland attacked Trahan's faulty memory by referring to her inconsistency in identifying Sullivan. He pointed out that Trahan had at one point testified that she did not get a good look at James Sullivan and yet later described him in detail. Recalling that Trahan had testified that Sullivan looked as if he had just stepped off a yacht; Garland referred to the prosecution's case as a mockery.

Garland described Harwood as pathological, a racist, violent, and a psychopath. He told the jurors that Harwood's oath should have been, "I, Tony Harwood, swear to lie."

Sullivan's other attorney, Don Samuel, focused on circumstantial evidence as well as the alleged inconsistencies and lack of corroboration in the prosecution's case. Samuel made reference to the prosecution's interpretation of Harwood being in possession of a piece of paper containing Sullivan's telephone numbers, contending that the prosecution had argued that the telephone numbers showed that Harwood and Sullivan were in contact with each other to plot the murder of Lita Sullivan. Samuel argued that it was just a piece of paper containing Sullivan's telephone number and that the paper was circumstantial, as was most of the prosecution's case. He told the jury that the prosecution's case was not only circumstantial, but without physical evidence. He then advised the jury that the only evidence that the prosecution had was Harwood, who was a liar. Samuel continued by reminding the jurors that not only was Harwood a liar, but that he had also lied to them.

TRIAL DAY NINE: FRIDAY, MARCH 10, 2006

After Judge Goger gave instructions to the jury, the deliberation phase of the trial began. Shortly afterward, the jury sent their first request for information to Judge Goger: wiretap recordings of conversations between Belinda Trahan and Anthony Harwood. The wiretap recordings made by the authorities had not been presented as evidence during the trial; therefore, Judge Goger denied the jury's request. The jury was apparently curious about the recordings because reference had been made to them numerous times during the trial.

Then, after fewer than five hours of deliberation, James Vincent Sullivan was convicted of all five counts of the indictment: murder, felony murder, aggravated assault (two counts), and burglary. Judge Goger had to call for silence in the courtroom when the guilty verdicts were being read.

The McClintons, who sat up front in the courtroom every day of the trial, held onto each other and began to weep as the verdicts were read. It was the end of a nearly twenty-year-long nightmare for them. Sullivan's conviction did not bring their daughter back to them, but I am reasonably sure that it did bring a sense of closure to the horrific events that took place on January 16, 1987.

I am sure that one of the most difficult things for the McClintons to endure was James Sullivan's arrogance, defiance, contempt, and lack of compassion regarding Lita's death. The McClintons continued to embrace each other as they released the anguish and burden they had been carrying for nearly twenty years.

Although I felt that what I had endured for the last twenty years was burdensome, I would rather have endured what I went through to infinity than to endure what the McClintons did. Justice had finally been served. Fulton Count District Attorney Paul Howard sat on the same bench as the McClintons as the verdicts were read. He said that justice had finally arrived, and also made reference to Belinda Trahan's courage in coming forward.

I personally have mixed feelings about Ms. Trahan. I feel that she should have been considered a conspirator, especially with all of the information that was available to her before Lita Sullivan was murdered. In my opinion, Trahan could have prevented the murder of Lita Sullivan by going to the authorities. But, in the back of my mind, I still wonder: would the authorities have ever solved this case if Trahan had not come forward? I don't know.

James Sullivan appeared to be trying to show no emotion, but the expression on his face suggested that he was visibly shaken by the verdicts. He was immediately ushered back to the holding cell adjacent to the courtroom. Defense attorney Don Samuel went back to the holding cell and spoke with him. When he returned from the holding cell, he announced that he would appeal Sullivan's conviction. He also said, "It takes a lot out of you to lose a murder trial, particularly a death penalty trial."

Many courtroom spectators were overjoyed to hear that Sullivan was found guilty of the murder of Lita McClinton Sullivan.

TRIAL DAY TEN: MONDAY, MARCH 13, 2006

During the penalty phase of the trial, Lita Sullivan's family members testified on her behalf. The family offered personal memories and times that they shared with Lita, and they told the court how James Sullivan had caused incalculable pain by having Lita killed. How James Sullivan selfishly took Lita Sullivan's life at the young age of thirty-five years by hiring a hit man to kill her, just to hold on to his money.

JoAnn McClinton gave the most moving testimony during the penalty phase. She told the court of a recurring dream that she had of her daughter. "She is always at a distance; I can see her, but I can never get to her. She is smiling and walking in my direction and I in hers, but we can never reach each other. I awake in chills, having a panic attack." This powerful testament brought some of the jurors to tears.

Mrs. McClinton wept and then continued, "Can I forgive him? No. Will I forgive him? No." She then added, "Time will not allow me to tell you what my family has gone through for the past nineteen years." Mrs. McClinton closed by saying, "I ask for justice for my daughter's killer. I have looked forward to this day for many years."

James Sullivan's brother Frank wanted to testify during the penalty phase—not on his brother's behalf, but against him. Judge Goger denied his request to testify, but later Frank Sullivan spoke with the media. He said that his brother was selfish and not a representative of the Sullivan family.

ADA Anna Green addressed the jury. "Nineteen years is too long to have no consequences for a crime as heinous as this." She added, "It is the defendant's actions that bring him here. It is the defendant's choices that snuffed out her life." ADA Green requested that the jury sentence Sullivan to death.

Two priests testified on Sullivan's behalf. Father John Brooks, president emeritus of College of the Holy Cross testified that Sullivan contributed or raised nearly $500,000 for the school over the course of the years. The second priest counseled Sullivan in jail while he was awaiting trial. He testified that Sullivan seemed to have a good relationship with Chongwattana Sriharoenmuang Reynolds, Sullivan's fourth or common-law wife. He also added that Sullivan appeared to be sincere and genuine.

Defense attorney Josh Moore told the jury that the Sullivan case did not warrant the death penalty and that life in prison for Sullivan would be equivalent to a death sentence. He said, "You don't need to kill James Sullivan to punish him. Your verdict has ensured that he will die in prison, and part of him is already dead." Moore reminded the jury that Sullivan would be in prison with rapists, murderers, and other violent felons who were younger and stronger than he. "It is not necessary to kill Jim Sullivan to honor Lita's memory," he said. "It is not necessary to kill Jim Sullivan to bring closure to this case and to this family. We don't need to strap him down to a gurney and inject him with lethal poison." Moore also told the jurors that Jim Sullivan's case was not a death penalty case, citing that Lita was not brutalized or tortured over days.

Don Samuel asked the jury to show mercy and compassion and to spare Sullivan from a death sentence. He urged them to choose life imprisonment for Sullivan.

Defense attorney Garland reiterated what had already been said by his colleagues, adding that God should decide the time for Sullivan to die.

ADA Kellie Hill told the jurors, "Life in any form is more than [Sullivan] allowed Lita to have. After he paid someone to take her life, how dare they ask to spare his life." Hill reminded the jurors that Lita Sullivan suffered for nearly an hour before she died. She argued that the death penalty was appropriate, stating: …"This defendant has lived his parole for nineteen years," referring to the length of time it took to bring him to justice.

CHAPTER 14: THE SENTENCING AND APPEAL

TRIAL DAY ELEVEN: TUESDAY, MARCH 14, 2006

After the jury heard the statements from the prosecution and defense and testimonies from Lita's family, they began deliberating on the fate of James Vincent Sullivan. Would it be death by lethal injection or life in prison without the possibility of parole? How would the jurors vote?

Soon after deliberations began, the jury sent a question to Judge Goger regarding a straight life sentence verses life without parole. The judge discussed the matter with the prosecution team as well as the defense team. ADA Green advised the judge to inform the jury that parole is a function of the Board of Pardons and Paroles and was not their concern. Attorney Don Samuel advised the judge that the jury should be told the truth, which is that the Board of Pardons and Paroles would not be able to release Sullivan under a straight life sentence before he had served fifteen years. The prosecution advised the judge that the parole guidelines could change at any time. Judge Goger agreed with the prosecution and told the jurors that a parole decision is within the exclusive discretion of the State Board of Pardons and Parole.

After discussing the parole issue, ADA Green told Judge Goger that she wanted it to become part of the record that Sullivan had declined to testify during the sentencing phase of his trial. Judge Goger then questioned Sullivan regarding his decision not to testify. Sullivan stood and said, "I didn't realize that I had the opportunity during the sentencing phase." The judge then advised Sullivan to take his time and confer with his counsel before deciding whether or not he wanted to testify on his own behalf. After conferring with his attorneys, Sullivan said that he did not want to take the stand.

At last, the jury emerged from the jury room. The jury foreperson handed the sentencing information to the bailiff who passed the documents to Judge Goger. The courtroom grew silent as Judge Goger reviewed the jury's decision. The judge then returned the documents to the bailiff and asked that they be entered into record.

The jury foreperson asked the judge which should be read first, and he told her to begin with the decision for the aggravated circumstances first. The courtroom was absolutely silent as the foreperson began reading Sullivan's sentence. "We, the jury, unanimously find beyond a reasonable doubt the existence of the following statutory aggravated circumstances. James Vincent Sullivan caused or directed another to commit the murder of Lita McClinton Sullivan. We, the jury, unanimously fix the sentence at life in prison without parole."

James Sullivan was indicted and convicted on the following charges:

1. Murder
2. Felony Murder
3. Aggravated Assault
4. Aggravated Assault
5. Burglary

The judge directed the bailiff to show the sentencing forms to defense counsel. Judge Goger instructed the jurors to retire to the jury room. He then asked to hear from the state regarding sentencing. ADA Green asked Judge Goger to merge counts 2 and 3 with count 1, and sentence Sullivan to twenty years on count 4, to run consecutive to count 1, and sentence him to twenty years on count 5, to run consecutive to any other sentence, for a total sentence of life in prison without parole, plus forty years. The judge then asked Sullivan if there was anything that he wanted to say before sentence was imposed, and he replied, "No, thank you." Defense attorney Ed Garland asked the judge to run the sentences concurrently in light of the sentence on the murder charge. Judge Goger did not respond to his request.

Before pronouncing sentence on Sullivan, Judge Goger said, "This has been a very long and difficult and horrible, horrible story." To Emory and JoAnn McClinton, he said, "Mr. and Mrs. McClinton, these lawyers did a very good job for you and for the memory of your daughter."

Judge Goger then addressed James Sullivan. "Mr. Sullivan, on count one you are sentenced to life in prison without the possibility of parole. Count two, I think the state is correct, merges into count one, as does count three. And in count four, you are sentenced to twenty years to run consecutive to the sentence imposed on count one. Count five you are sentenced to twenty years to run consecutive to the sentence imposed on count one and count four."

Sullivan tried to be stone-faced during the sentencing, but it was apparent that he was shattered, hearing that he would spend the rest of his natural life in prison—and for what? His greed for money and his willingness to take Lita's life to avoid sharing it. There is no way that it could have been worth it, not for all of his millions, not for nearly twenty years of freedom, some of which he was on the run. Sullivan looked despondent, lost in a daze, probably in denial—not of having Lita murdered, but in denial of the reality that he would have to spend the rest of his life in prison. Sullivan's spirit seemed finally to be broken, broken beyond repair.

The McClintons did not show a great deal of emotion during the sentencing, but hopefully they felt as if some form of justice had been served.

Judge Goger then asked, "Is there anything further?" When there was no reply, he said, "We're adjourned."

The deputies had gathered around Sullivan as he stood up slowly and spoke with his attorneys. He then walked over to one of the deputies and turned around to be handcuffed, and was led from the courtroom.

JoAnn McClinton, who at the time was a Georgia state representative, said that she was hoping for one thing—that he would be found guilty. She added that he thought he could get away with the murder of Lita because he had money.

After the trial, in an interview with NBC *Dateline*, Emory McClinton said, "We won the battle. He's not going to make a mockery of the court system anymore. It's over, Jim—Merry Christmas."

One of the jurors stated that the influence of religion played a part in the life sentencing instead of the death penalty. She added that the jury did not want to be the judge of someone's life.

Although Sullivan did not show much emotion during the course of the trial, his attorneys stated that he was relieved after the sentence. Attorney Garland said, "We are very thankful that the jury did not impose the death penalty."

Sullivan's attorneys reiterated that they would appeal his conviction.

THE APPEAL

On March 20, 2006, Sullivan's defense team filed a motion for a new trial, citing that the authorities had submitted an affidavit to the prosecution which contained false and deceptive information. The appeal was denied on August 30, 2006. Still committed to getting their client a new trial, the defense team filed an appeal to the Supreme Court of Georgia on September 5, 2006. The Court heard oral arguments on September 9, 2008, and on September 22, 2008, it unanimously upheld James Vincent Sullivan's conviction and denied a new trial.

∞

EPILOGUE

It took more than twenty years for justice to be served in the case against James Sullivan. Hopefully the McClintons felt some semblance of relief in knowing that the person responsible for their daughter's death had been convicted and will spend the rest of his life behind bars.

The twenty-year curse has officially ended.

Why did I consider it a twenty-year curse? I started nearly a dozen personal and business projects since I was considered a suspect in Lita's murder in 1987. This book is the first project that I have completed since 1987, thus signaling that the curse has ended. Every time I began a project, it would somehow be interrupted due to some aspect of the investigation.

During the Christmas season following the conclusion of the trial, I was listening to a song from the Mannheim Steamroller's *Christmas Celebration* CD. As the song, "Veni Veni," played, for some reason, all of a sudden I became very emotional and my eyes filled with tears. I did not know the English lyrics to the song, which is in Latin, but there was something about the bells that made it very dramatic. I knew that the words had to be very powerful to evoke such emotion. I began thinking about Lita and her parents, the McClintons, and all that they had endured for twenty years, as well as what my family and I had to deal with. There was something about the song that was telling me there was finally closure for the McClintons and that Lita was at peace. I listened to the song over and over. I then decided to find a translation for the lyrics, and the first one I came across seemed to be profound. The lyrics translate as follows:

"O come, O come, Emmanuel,
And ransom captive Israel,
That mourns in lonely exile here
Until the Son of God appear.

Refrain (Rejoice! Rejoice! Emmanuel
Shall come to thee, O Israel.)

O come, Thou Rod of Jesse, free
Thine own from Satan's tyranny:
From depths of hell Thy people save,
And give them victory o'er the grave. (Refrain)

O come, Thou Day-Spring, come and cheer
Our spirits by Thine advent here;
Disperse the gloomy clouds of night
And death's dark shadows put to flight (Refrain)

O come, Thou Key of David, come,
And open wide our heavenly home;
Make safe the way that leads on high,
And close the path to misery. (Refrain)

O come, O come, Thou Lord of Might,
Who to Thy Tribes on Sinai's height
In ancient times didst give the law
In cloud, and majesty, and awe. (Refrain)

I think to say anything more would be pointless.

THE END

For additional detailed information regarding the Lita Sullivan mur-der case, read the "Special Topic Section" that follows.

SPECIAL TOPIC SECTIONS

This book contains six special-topic sections, which cover specific topics and/or events in great detail. These special topic sections enable the reader to access more details on a specific topic at a later time, or at will, without interrupting his or her reading of the book.

Main Characters
Chronological Sequence of Events
Jim Sullivan's Philandering
Jim and Lita's Townhouse on Slaton Drive in Atlanta
Jim and Lita's Oceanfront Mansion in Palm Beach
The Wiretap Tape Recordings

MAIN CHARACTERS

JAMES VINCENT SULLIVAN

Sullivan is an Irish Catholic businessman who grew up on the south side of Boston. In the early 1970s, he moved to Macon, Georgia, to help his uncle operate a liquor distributorship. After the death of his uncle, Jim acquired the business.

Sullivan stood to lose a substantial part of his estate during his divorce to Lita. His estate included the Palm Beach mansion, which was valued at over $3 million; a $600,000 townhouse in Atlanta's exclusive Buckhead section, and other assets, in all totaling over $5 million. James Sullivan became the prime suspect immediately following the death of his second wife, Lita McClinton Sullivan.

LITA MCCLINTON SULLIVAN

Lita was an attractive, sophisticated, and intelligent African-American woman who attended a private school and then went on to Spelman College in Atlanta. She met Jim Sullivan while working at T. Edwards boutique in Atlanta. Jim was obsessed with winning Lita's heart. He showered her with gifts and was very persistent about developing a relationship. Although Lita's parents had reservations about Jim, Lita eventually married him. Just before the marriage, Lita was surprised when Jim presented her with a prenuptial agreement that was prepared by his attorney. Feeling pressured, and fearing that Jim would call off the wedding if she did not go along, Lita signed the agreement. After they were married, Lita moved to Macon, Georgia to live with her new husband. Jim did not want Lita to work, but she became actively involved with civic organizations and the Macon social arena.

Lita did not like the fact that she had had to give up her career. She soon realized that being married to Jim was not what she had expected. She was given a small allowance, which included money to buy groceries, gas, to go to the hair salon, and to buy personal items. Jim appeared to be extravagant socially, but when it came to his wife, he was miserly. If Lita ran out of money, she would have to account for the money that she had spent and all but beg Jim for more.

Jim began philandering, and he treated Lita with little or no respect, almost as if he resented the fact that they were married. After a few years, their relationship became strained due to Jim's cruel treatment. Lita would occasionally get fed up and stay in Atlanta for a few days, either at her parents' or with Poppy Finley Marable, her best friend and former Spelman College classmate. Jim would eventually call Lita and ask her to come home, or sometimes he would come to Atlanta for her. He would promise to give her more money and to be a better husband.

Unfortunately, things did not change for Lita, and she continually complained to Jim about the finances, his philandering, and the prenuptial agreement. Finally, Jim offered to increase Lita's allowance and to revise the agreement. This appeased Lita for a short while, but she realized that Jim had not changed; he continued womanizing and being disrespectful to her.

After Jim sold the liquor distributorship, they moved to Palm Beach. In addition to Jim's philandering and lack of respect, Lita now had to deal with the snobby Palm Beach crowd. One day, Lita was finally fed up with it all. While Jim was out of town on business, she hitched a U-Haul trailer to the back of her Mercedes, packed it with everything that would fit inside, and headed for their elegant townhouse in Atlanta. The next day, she filed for divorce in Atlanta, even though she and Jim were residing in Palm Beach, Florida.

After a year of hearings, motions, pleading, and depositions, Lita's divorce was far from being finalized. The legal fees had exceeded $100,000 and were still mounting.

POPPY FINLEY MARABLE

Poppy Finley Marable, an attractive, intelligent, and successful African-American woman and a long-time friend of Lita Sullivan. Poppy and Lita met during their years at Spelman College in Atlanta and became best friends. Their friendship faded somewhat after Lita moved to Palm Beach.

The two renewed their friendship after Lita returned to Atlanta and filed for divorce against her husband. Poppy's husband repeatedly warned her about spending so much time and sympathizing with Lita during the Sullivan divorce. Poppy continued to sympathize with Lita by going out at night with her and spending a great deal of time with her.

Poppy and Marvin separated, pending their divorce. Poppy retained Rick Schiffman, the same attorney that Lita was using for her divorce.

Poppy was in the house the morning that Lita was murdered and, with the exception of Lita's murderer, was the last person to talk with Lita.

CHRONOLOGICAL SEQUENCE OF EVENTS

1962 - Sullivan graduates from College of the Holy Cross.

1965 - Sullivan marries his first wife Catherine.

1971 - Marvin D. Marable is appointed a police officer in Mount Vernon, New York.

1973 - James Vincent Sullivan moves his family to Macon, Georgia, to help manage his uncle's liquor distributorship.

1973 - Marvin Marable is appointed a state trooper with the New York State Police.

1974 - Lita Sullivan and Poppy Finley graduate from Spelman College in Atlanta, Georgia.

1975 - James Sullivan inherits his uncle's liquor distributorship after his death.

1975 - Sullivan meets Lita McClinton while she is working in T. Edwards boutique in Atlanta.

1976 - Sullivan divorces his first wife Catherine; she returns to the Boston area in January with their four children.

1976 - Sullivan marries Lita McClinton on December 29th.

1977 - Marvin Marable graduates from Iona College in New Rochelle, New York and later moves to Chicago, Illinois.

1978 - Marable purchases a forty-four-unit apartment complex in Atlanta, Georgia.

1978 - Marable meets Lita's parents, Emory and JoAnn McClinton.

1978 - Marvin Marable meets Jim and Lita Sullivan.

1978 - Lita Sullivan introduces Marvin Marable to Poppy Finley.

1978 - Marable moves from Chicago to Atlanta.

1981 - James Sullivan borrows money from his company's pension fund and purchases the historic oceanfront Casa Eleda mansion in Palm Beach, Florida, on July 24th.

1982 - Marvin Marable marries Poppy Finley on May 8th.

1982 - Lita Sullivan finds a Christmas card from James Sullivan's mistress in December.

1983 - James and Lita Sullivan move to Casa Eleda in Palm Beach.

1983 - Marvin and Poppy Marable purchase a luxury home in the Sandy Springs neighborhood in a northwest suburb of Atlanta.

1984 – The Sullivans purchase a luxury townhouse in the Buckhead section of Atlanta.

1985 - Lita Sullivan leaves her husband and drives from Palm Beach to their townhouse while he is out of town on business. The next day, she files for a divorce (August).

1985 - Marvin Marable places a wiretap device on his home telephone in December and secretly records telephone conversations of Poppy and Lita.

1986 - Marable contacts James Sullivan's attorney, John Taylor, and advises him of the wiretap recordings (January).

1986 - Marable contacts James Sullivan and advises him of the wiretap recordings.

1986 - Marable advises Sullivan in February that he is going to remove the wiretap recording device from his telephone. James Sullivan pleads with Marable not to remove the recording device.

1986 - Poppy and Lita find the recording device in February and turn it over to the district attorney, with only one tape.

1986 - Poppy files for divorce against Marvin Marable in February, and uses Lita's attorney Rick Schiffman.

1986 - Marable sends forty tapes by courier to James Sullivan at his Palm Beach mansion.

1986 - Marable visits James Sullivan at the mansion in Palm Beach.

1986 - Sullivan returns the tapes to Marvin Marable via his attorney Jeffrey Bogart; however, five tapes are missing. Marable confronts Jeffrey Bogart and James Sullivan.

1986 - Marable breaks all ties and communication with James Sullivan in April.

1986 - Marvin Marable refuses to appear for one of James Sullivan's divorce hearings after being subpoenaed to appear.

1986 - Marable is indicted on a felony invasion of privacy charge by the Fulton County District Attorney. A deal is worked out by Marable's attorney Mike Mears: no conviction, no record; case expunged.

1986 - Phillip Anthony (Tony) Harwood delivers a piano to Sullivan's Palm Beach mansion on November 24th. Sullivan propositions Harwood to kill Lita Sullivan. Sullivan later mails Harwood two certified checks totaling $12,500.

1986 - The Marables' divorce is finalized on December 29th.

1987 - James Sullivan applies for a loan to pay off the note on the Palm Beach property; however, he is advised that Lita will also have to sign in order for the loan to be approved.

1987 - Someone knocks on Lita Sullivan's door at the townhouse between 4:00 a.m. and 6:00 a.m., on January 13th. Lita does not answer the door.

1987 - James Sullivan calls Marvin Marable at approximately 7:02 a.m. on January 13th, seeking information about Lita. Marable does not provide any information.

1987 - Phillip Anthony Harwood and two other subjects check into room 518 at the Howard Johnson Motor Lodge on Roswell Road on January 13th, at approximately 7:24 a.m. The trio is driving a white Toyota with North Carolina license plates.

7:44 a.m. James Sullivan receives a telephone call from room 518 of the Howard Johnson Motor Lodge.

1987 - Sullivan calls Bob Christenson at his office at 8:58 a.m. and again at 9:31, on January 13th. Christenson is living in the same townhouse development where Lita Sullivan lives. Sullivan inquires about suspicious persons and vehicles in the area.

1987 - James Sullivan places a call to room 518 of the motel at approximately 10:33 a.m., on January 13th. The call is made from the Palm Beach residence.

1987 - Belinda Trahan tells Harwood that roses will get a female to open the door.

1987 - James Sullivan's attorney cancels a videotaping of furnishings at the townhouse on January 15th.

1987 - Lita Sullivan talks with her mother JoAnn McClinton on January 15th and tells her about the incident on January13th. Lita tells her mother that Poppy and her daughter Ingrid will be spending the night with her.

1987 - Poppy Finley Marable and her daughter Ingrid spend the night with Lita Sullivan at the townhouse on January 15th.

1987 - One of Harwood's co-conspirators purchases a dozen pink roses from Botany Bay florist on Peachtree Road shortly after 8:00 a.m., on January 16th. The trio is driving a white Toyota.

1987 - Bob Christenson sees a suspicious man hurrying towards Lita's townhouse just after 8:00 a.m. on January 16th.

1987 - On January 16th, Lita is preparing to go to a property-settlement hearing regarding the validity of the postnuptial agreement. Someone rings Lita's door at approximately 8:15 a.m. to 8:20 a.m. Lita answers the door, Phillip Anthony Harwood hands her a box containing a dozen pink roses, then fires two shots from a 9 mm automatic handgun.

1987 - Lita Sullivan dies enroute to the hospital or shortly afterwards.

1987 - James Sullivan receives a telephone call at the Palm Beach mansion approximately forty minutes after Lita is shot. The call comes from a rest area in Suwanee, Georgia. The greeting is supposedly "Merry Christmas."

1987 - A memorial service is held for Lita Sullivan on January 19th. Jim Sullivan does not attend.

1987 - James Sullivan secures a $960,000 loan to pay off the balloon note on the Palm Beach property.

1987 - James Sullivan's attorney advises authorities that he passed a private polygraph examination.

1987 - Marvin Marable is advised of his fifth amendment rights by the Atlanta Police Department on February 5th inferring that he is a prime suspect in the murder of Lita Sullivan. Marable declines to be interviewed based on the advice of attorney Mike Mears.

1987 - James Sullivan meets Harwood and Belinda Trahan in a Florida diner. Sullivan gives Harwood $12,500, the balance of the payment for killing Lita Sullivan.

1987 - James Sullivan marries Hyo-Sook Choi (Suki) Rogers on September 15th.

1990 - Sullivan is involved in an automobile accident while his driver's license is revoked. He convinces or forces his wife Suki to tell authorities that she was driving. The plan backfires and they both receive probation. James Sullivan is sentenced to modified house arrest.

1990 - Suki Sullivan and James Sullivan are divorced on December 13th. She tells the authorities that Sullivan admitted to her that he had had Lita Sullivan killed.

1990 - Marvin Marable is subpoenaed to testify in front of a federal grand jury. On the advice of his attorney, Marable refuses to testify.

1990 - Marvin Marable moves to New York.

1991 - Lita's parents Emory and JoAnn McClinton file a wrongful death suit against James Sullivan in Florida.

1991 - FBI agents exercise a search warrant at Sullivan's Palm Beach mansion. Firearms are found, which violates Sullivan's probation.

1991 - FBI informant Johnny Austin Turner, a career criminal, tells the FBI that he has information that Marvin Marable was a conspirator in Lita Sullivan's murder.

1991 - Thomas Bruce Henley is arrested in connection with the murder of Lita Sullivan in September. Later he is released due to lack of evidence to proceed with a trial.

1991 - James Sullivan sells his Palm Beach mansion on December 18th for a reported $3.2 million and moves to a smaller home in the Boynton Beach area of Palm Beach County Florida.

1991 - Marvin Marable receives a telephone call from Mike Mears, advising him that he has been issued "use" immunity (forced immunity).

Marable is advised that if he does not cooperate with authorities, he could be arrested for contempt.

1991 - Marvin Marable meets with the authorities and tells them about the telephone call that he received from James Sullivan on January 13th, 1987.

1991 - Marable testifies in front of a federal grand jury.

1991 - Marable takes an FBI-administered polygraph test. The FBI informs him later that the polygraph test revealed deception.

1992 - James Vincent Sullivan is indicted in federal court in January for arranging the death of Lita McClinton Sullivan, through interstate commerce (long-distant telephone calls).

1992 - Marvin Marable testifies against Sullivan at his federal trial in November.

1992 - Judge Marvin Shoob dismisses the trial, citing lack of evidence, before the case goes to the jury.

1993 James Sullivan is convicted of firearms charges after being a convicted felon. Sullivan receives eighteen months' Community Control Incarceration (CCI) and forty-two months of probation.

1993 - Marvin Marable marries again and moves to the Quantico, Virginia area.

1993 - JoAnn McClinton is elected to the Georgia House of Representatives.

1994 - The McClintons win a wrongful death verdict against James Sullivan for approximately $4 million. The verdict is later overturned due to a statute of limitations ruling.

1997 - The Palm Beach mansion is sold by its current owner for approximately $13 million.

1997 - Fulton County District Attorney's Office begins to aggressively pursue the Lita Sullivan murder case.

1997 - James Sullivan moves to Costa Rica.

1998 - Belinda Trahan provides authorities with information implicating Anthony Harwood as a suspect in Lita Sullivan's murder.

1998 - Phillip Anthony Harwood is indicted for the death of Lita Sullivan on April 19th.

1998 - James Sullivan is indicted on June 26th for the murder of Lita Sullivan. Advised of the indictment via telephone by his attorney, Sullivan flees Costa Rica, eventually establishing residence in Thailand.

1999 - The Florida Supreme Court reverses its prior ruling on the two-year statute of limitations in the wrongful death case. The McClinton's $4 million verdict is upheld. James Sullivan and his money, however, have disappeared.

1999 - The Lita Sullivan murder case is aired on *America's Most Wanted*.

2001 - The FBI offers a $500,000 reward for information leading to the arrest and conviction of James Sullivan.

2001 - Someone in Thailand recognizes James Sullivan from media publicity and informs the authorities.

2002 - Harwood pleads guilty to voluntary manslaughter in a plea agreement. Harwood admits to being the shooter and agrees to testify against James Sullivan. (He will later recant his confession.)

2002 - On July 2, 2002, Sullivan is arrested in Thailand for the murder of Lita Sullivan. He initially agrees to waive extradition, but later changes his mind and decides to fight extradition.

2003 - James Sullivan loses his battle to fight extradition; but he appeals the decision to the high court in Thailand.

2003 - The McClintons file a civil suit against the Swiss banking firm Julius Baer and its director in Florida, charging the bank's conspiracy with a bank in Liechtenstein to funnel funds to Sullivan.

2003 - Harwood is sentenced to serve twenty years in prison on a plea agreement to avoid a possible death penalty sentence if convicted for the murder of Lita Sullivan.

2004 - The Thailand court of appeals upholds a lower court decision and Sullivan is extradited to the United States on March 26, 2004.

2004 - The authorities seek the death penalty against James Vincent Sullivan.

2004 - Sullivan's defense team issues a not-guilty plea on all five counts of the indictment.

2004 - Sullivan's defense team files a suit to have the charges against him dropped, citing double jeopardy from the 1992 federal trial.

2004 - The estate of Lita Sullivan files a suit against Sullivan's attorneys to stop them from using hidden assets for Sullivan's defense.

2004 - The estate of Lita Sullivan attempts to force James Sullivan into bankruptcy, being listed as the sole creditor. One count of the action is granted.

2005 - The Supreme Court of Georgia rules out Sullivan's appeal for double jeopardy.

2005 - The authorities exhume the remains of Sullivan's uncle, Frank Bienert, to determine the cause of death. Nothing suspicious is found.

2006 - Jury selection begins January 5th from a pool of approximately 450 prospective jurors.

2006 - Marvin Marable receives a call from ADAs Sheila Ross and Clinton K. Rucker advising him that he will be subpoenaed to testify in the upcoming trial.

2006 - Marvin Marable receives a letter from ADA Ross telling him that he *was not* considered a suspect in Lita Sullivan's murder.

2006 - ADA Rucker and investigator Frederick Hall visit Marable in Virginia to discuss the case and to serve him with a subpoena to testify as a witness for the prosecution.

2006 - James Vincent Sullivan's murder trial begins on February 28, 2006.

2006 - Sullivan is convicted on all counts on March 10, 2006.

2006 - Sullivan is sentenced to life in prison without the possibility of parole on March 14th.

2006 - Sullivan's attorneys file a motion for a new trial on March 20, 2006, claiming that the authorities submitted an affidavit to the prosecution that contained false and deceptive information. The appeal is denied on August 30.

2006 - Sullivan's attorneys file an appeal to the Supreme Court of Georgia on September 5.

2008 - The Supreme Court of Georgia hears oral arguments on the appeal on September 9th.

2008 - The Supreme Court of Georgia unanimously upholds Sullivan's conviction and denies a new trial on September 22nd.

JIM SULLIVAN WOMANIZING/PHILANDERING

Over the course of their marriage, Lita had become increasingly unhappy with Jim's behavior. Jim did not respect her; he would openly flirt with women at social events in her presence. He would also try to get telephone numbers for future conversations or follow-up meetings. Jim tried to act as if he were above everyone else and as if he were more intelligent and more successful than anyone else. His success appeared to create a false sense of authority for him.

Some women are willing to compromise themselves and be number two or perhaps even number three in someone's life, especially if they are wined, dined, and given fine gifts—and perhaps even money. The extramarital affair that drew the most attention was an affair that Jim had with Tanya Tanksley. The affair began while Jim was living on Nottingham Drive in Macon, Georgia, and continued after he moved to Palm Beach. Jim met her when she was about to walk into a store in Macon. Jim drove up and struck up a conversation with her. Ms. Tanksley testified that the affair lasted for about seven years. She admitted to having a sexual relationship with Sullivan in Macon, in Atlanta, and in the mansion in Palm Beach. Tanksley told authorities that Jim Sullivan would leave pre-paid tickets at the airport for her to fly to see him in Palm Beach.

Jim's first wife was white. The wives that followed were all minorities: Lita, African-American; Suki, Korean; and wife or common-law wife number four, Chongwattana Sriharoenmuang, Thai. Not only were all of his subsequent wives minorities, most of his affairs were reportedly with minorities. What does this mean? Perhaps nothing; or perhaps it meant that Jim felt that he could get away with such behavior with minority women. Or maybe he felt that he did not have to answer to minority women, because they were minorities. Only Jim Sullivan knows the answer.

Some studies show that *some* men with power or who feel they have power, have a strong desire for extramarital sexual relationships, even presidents of the United States. Perhaps they feel that they have made accomplishments or mastered challenges and need different challenges. And maybe this carries over to their personal relationships. Also perhaps some of these self-appointed powerbrokers want a sophisticated, intelligent, attractive spouse, but seek something different to satisfy their secret or not-so-secret sexual desires.

How and why did Lita tolerate Jim's flirting and womanizing/philandering? Lita would sometimes leave Jim and go to Atlanta and stay for a couple of days. Jim would either call her and ask her to come back to him, or he would go Atlanta and plead for her to come back to him. It was not unusual for Jim to give Lita very expensive gifts (probably in exchange for apologizing). One of the gifts is said to have been valued at many thousands of dollars. I remember one time Lita drove to Atlanta from Macon and complained to Poppy about Jim being tight with his money. She was upset because Jim would not give her enough money to manage their home in Macon.

Even with the expensive gifts and the lifestyle of the rich and famous, Lita was unhappy. The novelty of expensive gifts would soon wear off, and the affairs would continue. The usual sequence of an affair—getting caught, begging for forgiveness, promising not to do it again, and giving an expensive make-up gift—did not apply to Jim. Jim continued his behavior, business as usual. One can only imagine how Lita felt being out at social functions with Jim, and others in attendance being aware of his behavior. It was disrespectful and a slap in the face for her. Before Lita filed for divorce against Jim, I never heard her say anything negative about him, with the exception of him being a tightwad when it came to money to manage their home. On the contrary, Lita would proudly boast of Jim's accomplishments in a very respectful manner.

Finally, Lita had had enough of Jim's arrogance, philandering, and cruel treatment. In August of 1985, while Jim was out of town on business, Lita packed her things and drove to the townhouse in Buckhead. Shortly thereafter, she filed for divorce. Lita hired attorney Rick Schiffman, reportedly one of the top five divorce attorneys in Atlanta during that time.

JIM AND LITA'S TOWNHOUSE ON SLATON DRIVE IN BUCKHEAD

The townhouse on Slaton Drive was located in the upscale Buckhead neighborhood of Atlanta. The townhouses are located in a cloister of nine large, spacious, private garage townhomes called the Coaches. Some of the townhouses were attached and some were detached. They were actually very large houses that happened to be attached, perhaps for zoning purposes. The Sullivans' townhouse had four bedrooms and four baths. It was traditional in style and was professionally decorated. I remember Jim complaining about how much the interior decorator was charging. Apparently, he felt that ten percent of the cost of the furnishing and decorations was excessive. The furnishings were estimated to be worth at least $200,000. Jim and Lita had the townhome built between 1982 and 1984 at a cost of approximately $430,000. In 2003, the townhouse sold for $1.65 million.

JIM AND LITA'S OCEANFRONT MANSION IN PALM BEACH (CASA ELEDA)

Jim Sullivan was not born into wealth, but he was a shrewd businessman. He developed his inherited liquor distributorship into a flourishing business. In 1981, Sullivan borrowed money from the company's pension fund and purchased Casa Eleda, a historic oceanfront mansion in Palm Beach. The mansion was built between 1927 and 1929 of natural coquina stone accented with red brick. Jim purchased the mansion for approximately $1.9 million in 1981, but had some restoration work performed on the mansion that increased its value.

The 13,000-plus square foot mansion was designed by Swiss architect Maurice Fatio. The large entrance foyer had a combination tile and stone floor. There were five bedrooms and ten bathrooms, and a massive formal living room with a painted beamed ceiling that connected two of the wings. The large dining room with an arched cypress wood ceiling could accommodate nearly two dozen guests. There were two kitchens, a large "prep" kitchen for catering large meals or banquets, and a large regular kitchen. The prep kitchen was equipped with a pantry and stainless steel commercial appliances. The house was so large that it was broken into wings, built to two stories in some areas and one story in other areas. The high, ornate ceilings and tall arched windows made the rooms seem even larger. There was a rectangular courtyard enclosed by all four interior sides of the mansion. The courtyard had a pool, a veranda, a fountain, and statues. In 1983, Jim and Lita moved to what some have called the Beverly Hills of the Southeast.

One of my favorite features of the mansion was the tunnel that went under South Ocean Boulevard and opened onto a private beach on the Atlantic. At the end of the tunnel was a doorway that opened to an egress, approximately ten feet or more above the beach. An old wooden ladder was kept at the end of the tunnel to walk down to the beach. During one of the several visits that Poppy and I made to the Palm Beach mansion, we purchased a new aluminum ladder to replace the old wooden ladder.

Even after spending nearly $2 million on one of the finest properties in Palm Beach, Jim found out that he could not buy his way into the social circle of third- and fourth-generation millionaires and billionaires. Even though he served as chairman of the Palm Beach Preservation Board and attended many social events, he was not accepted in the way that he had anticipated. Some say that it was because he had an African-American wife. Lita was not accepted in the Palm Beach social circle as she had been accepted in Atlanta and Macon. But after Lita was murdered, Sullivan married Suki, also a minority.

THE WIRETAP TAPE RECORDINGS

One day, I discovered a copy of a letter that Poppy had written to her attorney. In the letter Poppy had outlined what she wanted in a divorce settlement against me. My concerns about Poppy spending so much time with Lita were founded. Now I became suspicious of all of Poppy's activities. I began questioning her about going out so much, but she continued to deny any wrongdoing. I did not blame Lita for any of Poppy's actions; each individual is responsible for their own actions, including me.

Having previously worked as a cable-splicing technician for the New York Telephone Company and also as an investigator with the New York State Police while assigned to the Drug Enforcement Administration Task Force, I decided to do a little investigating on my own. I went to a Radio Shack store in Decatur, Georgia, and purchased a recording device. I specifically asked the salesman if it was legal for me to place the device on my home telephone to intercept telephone calls. The salesman told me that it was. I also purchased a cassette recorder and some cassette tapes. I took the device home and connected it to a telephone jack in the basement. I placed some boxes and other items in front of the device to conceal it from view. I tested the device to make sure it was working properly. I played back the tape and it had recorded my voice. The device was activated by sound, and the phone ringer would activate the system before the phone was answered.

I typically used 120-minute tapes, which allowed for sixty minutes of recording on one side before the tape stopped. The recorder did not have an automatic reverse feature, therefore the tape would have to be manually turned over to begin recording on the other side.

When I returned home at the end of the day, I would retrieve the tape and put a new one in the recorder. The next day I took the retrieved tape with me to listen to on another cassette player. I made written notes regarding some of the tapes' contents.

Poppy and Lita talked on the telephone nearly every day. They'd discuss Lita's impending divorce, and Lita would update Poppy on the latest developments. They would also talk about their weekend plans, going to parties, and going out of town. And of course, "girl talk." Poppy and Lita were truly the best of friends.

One day, I was playing back one of the tapes and I heard Poppy tell Lita that she was still considering divorcing me. Apparently, Poppy had previously discussed divorcing me with Lita. Now my suspicions were confirmed even more.

Lita would often come and visit us. Occasionally, she would use our telephone because she assumed that the telephone at the Buckhead townhouse was bugged. (Suki Sullivan, James Sullivan's third wife, stated that he told her that Lita was having a lot of sex, according to the tapes. I do not recall any conversations of Lita's that made reference to her having sex with anyone.) During conversations between Poppy and Lita, Lita would occasionally mention the name of someone she went out to dinner with or had met. During that time, Lita was legally separated from Jim.

The authorities and media later speculated that there was something on the tapes that drove Jim Sullivan to having Lita killed. I do not buy that. First of all, I listened to all of the tapes, and in my opinion, there was nothing on the tapes that would compel anyone to murder. What could compel anyone to murder anyway? Jim Sullivan listened to the tapes in the early spring of 1986. Lita was killed in January of 1987, more than eight months later. Jim Sullivan contracted Harwood to kill Lita in November of 1986, and he told him that he wanted the job done before Christmas of the same year. Why? In my opinion, Jim wanted Lita killed to avoid sharing his estate with her. Jim's panicked efforts, just days before Lita's death, convinced me that he wanted Lita killed in order to hold on to his money. Lita was killed just hours before the hearing to rule on the postnuptial agreement in her divorce case. By law, with Lita's death, Jim Sullivan retained all rights to his estate. What compels a person to commit murder? Their own twisted internal motivations, not the contents of a tape recording.

I contacted Jim's attorney John Taylor in January of 1986 regarding possible representation in my seemingly inevitable impending divorce. During my conversation with Taylor, I mentioned that I had been wiretapping my home telephone. He told me that Jim Sullivan would be interested in hearing the tapes.

I contacted Sullivan in February of 1986 and told him that I would be removing the wiretap device from my telephone. He all but begged me to leave it on the telephone for a little while longer, and promised to pay me $30,000 if he did not have to pay any more money or assets as indicated in Lita's postnuptial agreement. Against my better judgment, I agreed; and that turned out to be a big mistake. Shortly afterward, Lita and Poppy discovered the wiretap device. I sometimes wonder if Jim somehow informed Lita and Poppy of the recording device on the telephone. If he did, what would be his motivation? Perhaps this was part of his grand scheme? As mentioned elsewhere in the book, I never received any money from Jim Sullivan. After I broke off all ties with Sullivan in the spring of 1986 (due to the missing tapes), I wanted nothing to do with him or his money.

Why would I share the tape recordings with Jim Sullivan? It was more of a strategy than anything else. During that time, Lita was alive and I had no idea that Jim Sullivan would have her murdered. It is not unusual for individuals to share information in their divorces, but it is unusual for someone to be murdered. Contrary to the belief of some people, neither Jim nor his attorneys approached me to place the recording device on the telephone; it was all my idea. When I placed the recording device on my telephone in December of 1985, no one else had knowledge of my actions. The device was placed on my home telephone to intercept Poppy's telephone calls; Lita's calls were incidental to my original intent.

I was upset because Poppy and Lita seemed to be plotting together to divorce Jim and me. Poppy and Lita must have felt that there was information on the tapes that could have been used against them during their divorces. Poppy and Lita confronted me at a car dealership one day and made an unsuccessful attempt to retrieve the tapes. It is not necessarily what they said on the tapes but what they think they might have said; it would be very difficult to remember what you said on the telephone for more than two months. The tapes served more as leverage for me than as a liability for either Poppy or Lita.

I also mentioned that I mailed the tapes to Jim Sullivan by courier. Jim reneged on his agreement and did not return all of the tapes to me. I disposed of the tapes in a dumpster in South Dekalb County one evening, shortly after being indicted by the Fulton County District Attorney's Office. The one tape that was turned in to the authorities was innocuous and did not contain any recorded conversations. There were also issues of legal interpretation pertaining to wiretap laws, ownership, and chain of custody. Fortunately, the felony wiretap indictment case against me was disposed of without a criminal conviction or record of a criminal conviction.

SOURCES

A great deal of the information contained in this book comes from my own personal knowledge; however, some information was obtained from newspaper articles, internet news articles, court documents, and other sources. While researching the book, I discovered numerous discrepancies widely reported in the media, especially pertaining to the dates and times of certain events. I made every effort to verify the accuracy of all information contained in the book.

∞
ABOUT THE AUTHOR

Marvin D. Marable was born in rural Halifax County, Virginia. He moved to White Plains, New York, in Westchester County, when he was six years old. Later, his family moved to Mount Vernon, New York. Marvin graduated from Mount Vernon High School. He served in the Army and Army National Guard as a commissioned officer. He served in an infantry unit and a military police unit.
Marvin was a police officer for the Mount Vernon Police Department for several years and was later appointed a state trooper with the New York State Police. While serving with the state police, Marvin was assigned to the Drug Enforcement Administrations (DEA) Task Force. Injured while serving on the task force, Marvin eventually retired from the state police.

A graduate of Iona College in New Rochelle, New York, Marvin has a degree in criminal justice. He lived briefly in Chicago before moving to Atlanta, where he became a government contractor and also invested in commercial and residential real estate.

It was in Atlanta that Marvin met Jim and Lita Sullivan and his first wife, Poppy Finley Marable.

Marvin is currently writing another book entitled *A State Trooper's Log (9125 To Hawthorne)*. Visit the author's website at *deadlyroses.com or gccillc.com.*

9477990R0012

Made in the USA
Charleston, SC
16 September 2011